W9-CBA-212

Paul Domjan • Gavin Serkin
Brandon Thomas • John Toshack

Chain Reaction

How Blockchain Will Transform the Developing World

Paul Domjan
NormannPartners
London, UK

Gavin Serkin
New Markets Media & Intelligence
London, UK

Brandon Thomas
Grayline Group
Austin, TX, USA

John Toshack
Delphos International
London, UK

ISBN 978-3-030-51783-0 ISBN 978-3-030-51784-7 (eBook)
https://doi.org/10.1007/978-3-030-51784-7

This Palgrave Macmillan imprint is published by the registered company Springer Nature Switzerland AG.
The registered company address is: Gewerbestrasse 11, 6330 Cham, Switzerland

Chain Reaction

For all those pursuing a post-kleptocratic world in which transparency keeps us honest and includes the excluded.

Foreword

There is a growing realization all over the world, but particularly in developing countries, that there is a set of problems linked to trust, verification and value transfer that could actually be solved with blockchain technology, unlocking untold potential for advancement.

This is the starting point for *Chain Reaction*. In this sense it is very much an emerging markets book, which is why I found it so interesting. Yet, in taking the reader on a journey—often in some of the world's most challenging regions—to where one of the most transformative technologies is being applied, it is also incredibly helpful for anyone who truly wants to understand why people are so excited by what is often described as little more than an accounting tool or fancy spreadsheet.

Step by step, the authors explain with clarity the essential tenets of how Bitcoin works, how other blockchains overlap and differ from Bitcoin, and how entrepreneurs in developing countries are adopting this technology in an attempt to solve a multitude of problems from money transfer to counterfeit prescription drugs, holding warlords to account and testing for coronavirus. Case studies from Uganda to the Philippines and Mongolia, along with useful developed world examples, serve to emphasize the massive impact the concepts so far proven by Bitcoin could have on the developing world.

These practical examples also tackle the significant challenges for blockchain, and for Bitcoin in particular, such as gaining acceptability in entrenched industries, issues around data integrity and the resistance of governments who fear loss of power and control with blockchain adoption. Blockchain is not the panacea that cures all ills.

In consideration of such obstacles, the authors review the development of mobile wallets and payment systems, as exemplified by M-Pesa in Kenya and

WeChat in China. Most interestingly, they show how the frontier markets of Africa, despite lower per capita wealth—or perhaps because of this—are among the most innovative in the world and are successfully "leapfrogging" into latest technologies.

The chapter on trust is especially insightful, looking at the problems created in property records as a significant example. The authors explain how risk can be mitigated through a blockchain's ability to simplify verification and leverage transparency to develop trust, if managed effectively. Another chapter shows an aid organization using blockchain to distribute vouchers that can be used as electronic cash, with the advantage of being able to accurately and efficiently trace each user and their transactions.

The authors take care to explain blockchain in a way that is both accessible to the novice but with sufficient depth to comprehend the considerable issues that the technology is grappling with. The book also acknowledges that even the language used to describe these emerging technologies is in flux, as the authors explain what is (and is not) meant by "decentralized", "trustless" and other adjectives often thrown around to describe blockchain-based systems. Hint: these words don't mean what you think they mean.

One innovative idea coherently explained is the possibility of private permissioned blockchains, with a "proof of stake" validation and consensus mechanism, where validators deposit money and use it as collateral to vouch for a block in the blockchain, providing a useful half-way house between fully decentralized public chains and centralized legacy systems. In probing how blockchains operate and who controls them, we get to know the various actors: the users, node operators, miners and developers—the people who maintain and create the protocols on which these systems run.

Chain Reaction takes us beyond the binary excitable view of cryptocurrencies where bull market ideologues face off against gold-bugs and sceptics who decry crypto as worthless, in favor of a more considered exploration of cryptocurrencies vis-à-vis their competition, ranking their qualities in comparison to physical and electronic cash. Crypto comes out poorly, for now, as an accepted means of exchange, but beats physical cash for storage and, crucially for emerging markets, immunity to the hyper-inflation, capital controls and banking sector risks that plague many fiat currencies. This leads us to the book's central thesis: if the potential of blockchain technology is to be fulfilled, developing markets are likely to be the biggest beneficiaries.

Overall, this book provides not only a wonderful insight into how blockchain can impact the developing world but is also a primer for understanding distributed leger technology, blockchain and cryptocurrencies.

Dubai, United Arab Emirates Mark Mobius

Mark Mobius is the former Executive Chairman of Templeton Emerging Markets Group, and Founding Partner of Mobius Capital Partners.

Contents

1 Introducing Blockchain: Tomorrow's Railroads 1

2 Trust Matters 9

3 What Does Blockchain Solve? 15

4 Who Really Controls Blockchain? 25

5 Making Money 45

6 More than Money 57

7 Opening Up Trade 79

8 The Big Bet Vs. Devil You Know 93

Conclusion 101

Index 105

List of Figures

Fig. 1.1	Global product and process innovation: percentage of firms introducing new products and new processes by region	6
Fig. 2.1	Index measuring the quality of property registration institutions globally	12
Fig. 2.2	Contract enforcement: days to enforce and cost of enforcement as a percentage of contract value	13
Fig. 4.1	Bitcoin price	26
Fig. 4.2	Secure Hashing Algorithm 256 (SHA256) in practice: the hash of "Hello World" vs. the hash of "Hello Worl"	30
Fig. 4.3	Antminer S9 13.5 TH/S Bitcoin Miner	32
Fig. 4.4	Time since each bitcoin was last transacted	33
Fig. 4.5	Blockchain vs. a directed acyclic graph, or DAG	39
Fig. 6.1	Tax revenue as a percentage of GDP across various economies	74
Fig. 7.1	Example of counterfeit medicine	80
Fig. 7.2	Ease of trading across borders score	87

1

Introducing Blockchain: Tomorrow's Railroads

Why do some innovations succeed while others fail? How can we predict which will succeed and when? Why do some innovations seem to explode onto the scene while others build slowly? Why are some innovations credited with making the world a better place, while others seem to create new problems faster than they solve old ones? These aren't easy questions to answer, which is why venture capitalists spread their risk across a wide array of innovations rather than relying on the instincts of a small number of entrepreneurs.

While we may not be able to predict which innovation will succeed, there are some principles that help us understand what success is and isn't. Let's begin at the point where an innovation has been developed, has found some early adopters and has made its first tentative steps towards commercialization. It is at this stage that many innovations tend to get stuck, while others spread rapidly and disrupt existing industries.

To move beyond this initial phase, an innovation must be "good enough" to meet the needs of a particular market. Innovations tend to attract wider adoption when the new thing is good enough to replace the existing thing. The new doesn't need to replicate all the features of the existing. In fact, the new will tend to be much better in some new attributes, while only minimally effective in other attributes.[1] One key driver for innovations to encroach upon the existing is the market environment. Alternative systems can take root faster and with less overhead the less developed the status of existing systems.

[1] Christensen, Clayton M. 1997. *The Innovator's Dilemma: When New Technologies Cause Great Firms to Fail.* Boston, MA: Harvard Business School Press.

P. Domjan et al., *Chain Reaction*, https://doi.org/10.1007/978-3-030-51784-7_1

Numerous examples demonstrate how innovations have stalled in developed economies, only to thrive in the developing world—perhaps most famously in the case of mobile money. M-Pesa, first launched in Kenya in 2007, is one of the earliest and best-known mobile money wallets. Starting first as a means to make payments using Nokia-type handsets, M-Pesa has inspired multiple similar operations throughout the developing world, particularly among lower-income users where bank account penetration is low.[2]

> From Paul: When teaching MBA classes five or six years ago, I would ask students to raise their hand if they'd used mobile payments in the past month. At that time, nobody in a lecture theater in the US or the UK had used mobile payments. In fact, the first time that I used a mobile wallet in my daily life in London was because I'd left my physical wallet at home. The same question asked across Africa or parts of Asia would have triggered an almost unanimous show of hands.

So why was mobile money "good enough" for Kenya, but not the UK or US? M-Pesa launched in June 2007, a month before the iPhone. When M-Pesa really took off in 2011, using mobile money was still a pretty awful experience. The rich mobile app experiences the iPhone would ultimately create had yet to take over our wallets. Mobile money at that time was based on exchanging credit balances held by the mobile network, not a bank. It didn't generate interest or benefit from any sort of deposit protection. Users were unable to get credit, as with a credit card. Transactions were cumbersome and clunky, effected through sending texts with complicated transaction codes to direct the movement of funds. Why would someone with access to a credit card or a bank account use a system that had fewer benefits than a bank and was more difficult to use than a credit card?

The answer lies in the concept of being "good enough." While mobile money was much weaker than the system of credit cards, it had attributes that made it much more attractive in developing countries. For one thing, you didn't need a bank account or credit history—services that are hard to come by in rural Kenya, particularly for informal workers lacking the right documents. For merchants, point-of-sale terminals for credit cards at the time required a physical telephone connection, a costly piece of infrastructure that could take weeks or even months to install; M-Pesa was accessible using the Nokia or equivalent basic phone that every merchant already had. Faced with constant risk of robbery, M-Pesa provided an attractive alternative to carrying and storing cash. These features—no bank account, credit history or landline required, and less need to carry cash—were more highly

[2] Shah, Rahul, et al. 2019. *The Digital Banking and Tech Revolution in EM.* Tellimer. https://insights.tellimer.com/article/the-digital-banking-and-tech-revolution-in-em. Accessed 1 April 2020.

prized in the developing world, enabling mobile money, as clunky as it was, to grow and thrive.[3]

> From Gavin: During a visit in 2017 to China's Guangxi region, famed for cone shape mountains set against the Li River, I found myself in a restaurant with little cash, only credit cards. I presented them one by one as my server shook her head. "Cash or WeChat," she repeated. In the hope of sparing me a long night of washing up, the server took me to every shop and restaurant in the street to see if they would take payment by my Visa or Mastercard, and then transfer my payment by WeChat to the restaurant. Half an hour and 25 vendors later, we returned to the restaurant. I promised to come back the next day with cash. Not one vendor accepted credit cards, only WeChat.

China took mobile money several steps further. Helped by the nascency of many of China's institutions and expansive economy, platform developers mashed mobile money with messaging, e-commerce and other digital trends—the most defined example being WeChat. This one platform represents a Cambrian explosion of multiple innovations (most incubated in more developed economies) coming together as one. No platform in the US, UK or other developed markets has come close to replicating the breadth of features offered by WeChat, nor the rate of penetration WeChat enjoys within the Chinese economy.[4] Both WeChat and Alipay now even have versions accepting payment via Visa or Mastercard for foreign visitors.

In Kenya, M-Pesa did not displace credit cards or bank accounts, but developed in tandem. This idea of innovations paralleling existing systems is commonplace.

> From Brandon: Retail is another clear example of an emergent system paralleling existing ones. Amazon and the broader e-commerce industry is quickly encroaching upon bricks and mortar retail in the US and other western economies, particularly since the coronavirus lockdowns. However, physical retail is not going away entirely. Even Amazon is opening physical stores. Why? Because what is evolving is no longer a binary bricks vs. clicks. What is developing is more an interplay between the emerging system and the incumbent. What is afoot is a reordering of the features that consumers value. Brand experiences are more important than direct in-store sales. For instance, you can buy an iPhone at your local Apple store, but that is not its main function; rather the store is a venue where anyone can have an Apple experience. It is designed to appeal to non-customers as much as customers.

[3] Mbele, Lerato. 2016. Why M-Pesa Failed in South Africa. *BBC Africa Business Report*, 11 May. https://www.bbc.com/news/world-africa-36260348. Accessed 26 December 2018.

[4] Chan, Connie. 2015. When One App Rules Them All: The Case of WeChat and Mobile in China. Andreessen Horowitz, 6 August. https://a16z.com/2015/08/06/wechat-china-mobile-first/. Accessed 12 February 2019.

Leapfrogging Through History

Before M-Pesa or WeChat, mobile phones themselves created at least double the additional productivity in developing countries as in advanced economies, despite the fact that they were rolled out much later in the developing world. To understand why, consider the system that mobiles replaced in the US compared with India, for example. Before mobiles, Americans would fumble for change at a pay phone or wait to go back to their home or office to make a call. In rural India, someone without access to a fixed-line phone might have to travel for hours for a conversation.

The efficiency of communication spawned by mobile phones levelled the playing field among developed and developing economies alike. Fishermen in the US Gulf of Mexico have a long history of using radio to work out which harbours to dock at to achieve the best price for their catch; mobile phones enabled fishermen in the Bay of Bengal to do the same.[5]

Mobile phones are the classic example of "technology leapfrogging," where economies can skip intermediate technology (landline telephony) and move straight to cutting edge tech. Mobile money is proving to be a similar case for financial inclusion in countries underserved by their banks. While banks in developed countries are closing branches to adapt to online banking, developing countries are able to deepen their financial systems, skipping the buildout of nationwide branch banking systems all together. The leapfrogged economy is freed of the operating and capital cost of offsetting the legacy system.[6]

Leapfrogging has occurred throughout post-industrial history, and before. Going back to the nineteenth century, railways were built in the richest countries long before poorer ones, but they provided a bigger incremental improvement in developing countries that lacked a pre-existing system of long-distance roads and canals. Where such networks existed, railroads offered higher capacity and speed. Where canal systems and major roads had not been constructed,

[5] For more details on the usage of mobile phones in the Indian fishing industry, see https://www.ictworks.org/surprise-fishermen-using-mobile-phones-for-market-prices-is-the-largest-lie-in-ict4d and Steyn, Jacques. 2016. A Critique of the Claims about Mobile Phones and Kerala Fisherman: The Importance of the Context of Complex Social Systems. *The Electronic Journal of Information Systems in Developing Countries* 74(3): 1–31.

[6] International Finance Corporation. 2018. *Digital Access: The Future of Financial Inclusion in Africa.* https://www.ifc.org/wps/wcm/connect/region__ext_content/ifc_external_corporate_site/sub-saharan+africa/resources/201805_report_digital-access-africa.

trains opened the possibility of long-distance overland transport for the first time.

In the same way that prior to mobile and railroads, telephone and transportation infrastructure was weaker in developing countries, today's equivalent lies in transactions infrastructure—the networks of accountability and trust that connect economic activity. Institutions of trust—the holders of public records such as land registries and licensing agencies—tend to be weaker in the developing world. Institutions are frequently less reliable, more cumbersome to use or, indeed, non-existent.

Of course, in the same way that it would be misleading to generalize about advanced economies, developing countries are far from homogeneous. The World Bank Enterprise Surveys show that 11% of firms in Italy experience bribery requests, a great deal more than in many developing countries, such as Turkey, Chile or Georgia. In European Union member state Hungary, firms expect to pay bribes amounting to 14.1% of the value of the contract to secure government work, more than in every country the World Bank surveys apart from Timor-Leste and Sierra Leone. Overall, though, about a quarter of firms operating in emerging and frontier markets report experiencing bribery requests, compared to less than 1% in developed countries.[7]

Enter Blockchain

Where existing institutions of trust are weak, it is easier for blockchain-based systems to be "good enough"—to offer an attractive alternative to existing approaches. It seems rational to expect such innovation—as with mobile phones, mobile money and railroads—to have the biggest impact in developing countries.

One further reason is that innovations tend to be deployed faster and with a more fundamental impact in places where there is a less entrenched way of doing things. The World Bank's Enterprise Surveys show that around a third of firms in Latin America and sub-Saharan Africa, and half of those in South Asia improved their processes from the prior year. In high-income countries, less than 7% had improved processes. Similarly, while 40% of firms in high-income countries introduced a new product to the market since the previous year, 74% of sub-Saharan African firms had done so. Liberia, Mongolia and

[7] https://www.enterprisesurveys.org/en/data/exploretopics/corruption.

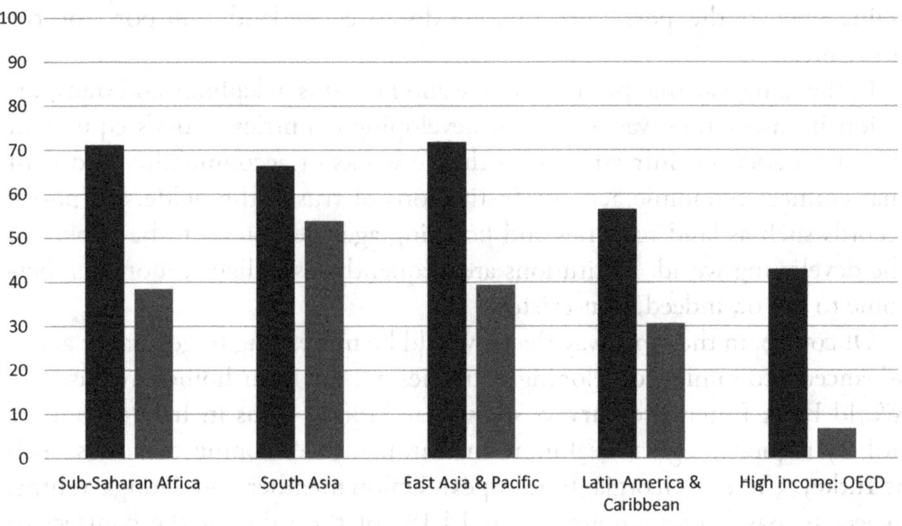

Fig. 1.1 Global product and process innovation: percentage of firms introducing new products and new processes by region. Source: World Bank Enterprise Surveys

Thailand stand out as examples of particularly strong product innovators, while Rwanda, Uganda and Papua New Guinea are strong process innovators (Fig. 1.1).[8]

None of this means that blockchain is destined to transform developing countries. The hype and hysteria around this innovation have been frothy, to say the least. Proponents advocate that it will revolutionize finance, supply chains, healthcare and more, and that Bitcoin will replace money and gold as a store of value: "Long bitcoin, short the bankers!"[9] As with most innovations pitched at this decibel level, reality falls short. For now at least, we still have bankers.

Like mobile money, in its purest form blockchain is fundamentally about creating networks over which transactions can be executed between parties unknown to one another. That's the starting point. Blockchain's particular innovation lies in making the parties to transactions truly sovereign: many public blockchain-based systems do not require any third party to provide services or permission at any point.

[8] https://www.enterprisesurveys.org/en/data/exploretopics/innovation-and-technology.

[9] https://twitter.com/APompliano/status/1045088576533405702.

To build such a system (and many had tried before) the problem that needed to be solved was "trust." The pseudonymous Satoshi Nakamoto published a paper entitled *Bitcoin: A Peer-to-Peer Electronic Cash System* in October 2008 that presented a novel combination of technologies to address this issue.[10] Trust between total strangers was to be achieved by combining elements of computer science, cryptography, game theory and economics. It created a paradigm within which participants were economically motivated towards good or honest behavior while bad actors were monitored and neutralized.

More than a decade on from the Bitcoin whitepaper, the blockchain ecosystem has developed at pace, with the community pursuing relentless and often chaotic experimentation under the mantra of "move fast and break things."[11] Since 2015 we have seen new methods of fundraising driving billions of dollars invested—and billions lost—in blockchain technology. The industry spawned a multitude of unregulated trading venues for a myriad cryptocurrencies. Thousands of whitepapers espouse every imaginable blockchain use case.

So far, few of these developments made the world a meaningfully better place. The crypto community itself has tribalized around different technologies and philosophical approaches to blockchain. Its silos and fiefdoms run counter to the decentralized idyll envisioned over a decade ago.

We have no desire to add to the hype nor advocate a single approach. In this book, we apply a broad definition of what constitutes "a blockchain." Our usage encompasses all of what many people would correctly refer to as distributed ledger technology or "DLT," being any networked system that has distributed record keeping and allows all users within the system to verify data. In this sense, a blockchain is essentially just a shared database. This extends the scope of discussion to systems and technologies where information is open and searchable in a shared ledger, even if they don't have some of the elements needed to meet purist definitions of what constitutes a blockchain.

What is clear is that for developing economies, and especially the smaller frontier markets, the traditional institutions of trust that might be relied upon in more advanced economies are frequently compromised by inaccessibility, under-funding, opacity and corruption—characteristics that undermine their role as arbiter of truth. Against this backdrop, the new paradigm of transparency made possible by blockchain provides an opportunity for systems to

[10] https://bitcoin.org/bitcoin.pdf.

[11] https://hbr.org/2019/01/the-era-of-move-fast-and-break-things-is-over.

emerge that rethink and redefine trust. In this context, for much of the developing world, the bar is lower for what constitutes "good enough."

Is this new paradigm already in existence? Can we see pockets of how these emerging technologies are providing "good enough" alternatives to existing systems?

The answer is an emphatic "yes." In this book, we explore how blockchain has helped bring the first banking services to rural communities in the Philippines, spurred intra-African trade by obviating the need for currency transactions to go via the US dollar, and created transparency on invoices to help Latin American farmers and small businesses obtain credit.

Other applications remain untested, niche or heroically ambitious—such as using evidence stored on the blockchain to prosecute presidents for war crimes. Still, these applications allow us to frame an analysis of the likelihood and speed of innovation and, from there, the potential impact of blockchain in the developing world.

This book argues that blockchain is a catalyst for the next epoch of technology leapfrogging. If harnessed correctly, regions so far left behind by global economic development can leverage these emergent systems to boost productivity, economic activity and overall quality of life. As with fixed-line phones, canals and trunk roads in the past, nascent economies can forgo the development of transaction and trust infrastructure.

The implications of this are profound. Populations living under corrupted regimes can hope for a new path of economic transparency by employing decentralized systems. Consumer credit could unleash untold reductions in poverty and lift welfare and living standards.

Yet, a positive outcome is by no means certain. As we will explore, blockchain-based record keeping carries risks of entrenching the problems of emerging markets rather than resolving them. With great power comes great responsibility.

2
Trust Matters

Trust is the oil that lubricates the global economy. When we pay for something, the merchant releases the goods because she trusts the value of the mechanism we have used to pay—whether that's paper money or a credit card. When we buy a house, we're willing to part with our hard-earned cash because we trust the registration documents provided by the seller as proof that the seller owns the house and has the right to sell it to us. When an investor buys a company's bonds, they rely on a wider circle of trusted inputs—a grade from an established credit ratings agency to help assess financial risk that the bonds represent, reports from the company's auditors for assurance that the company's finances are in order.

Consider the institutions of trust in these examples. The merchant only accepts our paper money because it is backed by the central bank—indeed she is legally compelled to accept its value. She accepts a credit card not because she is legally compelled to do so, but rather because the card is issued by a trusted network such as Visa or Mastercard with a long history of settling transactions. Ownership of the house is established by the land registry and various legal searches. When applying for a loan, the bank validates our income through statements or tax records and uses an independent credit records bureau to ensure that we are not already overburdened with debt. When engaging a supplier, a company relies on international standards certification (e.g. ISO), which in turn depends on trusted certification bodies, and on the effectiveness and integrity of the legal system to enforce contracts.

In every transaction, the parties trust a series of intermediaries, lessening the need to trust one another directly. Even accounting for occasional high-profile failures, these institutions are seen to offer generally reliable assessments. These intermediaries did not appear overnight. In developed economies,

P. Domjan et al., *Chain Reaction*, https://doi.org/10.1007/978-3-030-51784-7_2

the web of institutions and regulations intrinsic to any transaction evolved over decades or centuries. In developing countries, there is often a shorter expanse of time behind the trust in their institutions.

These webs of trust are living organisms, changing and iterating as failures occur, new needs arise and technology moves on. Where effective and efficient systems already exist, the bar is higher for establishing new systems, and their impact may be more constrained. In developing economies, more nascent arbiters of trust provide opportunity for alternative models to emerge. Many people do not have access to banks. Standards bodies are sometimes corrupted or ineffective. Contracts might be worth little more than the paper they are printed on. In some places, credibility of the national currency is perpetually at risk from inflation, exchange rate instability or restrictions on conversion to dollars.

From Paul: Even people who use dollars don't completely trust them. Often only crisp ones are accepted in places where access to banking is limited. This realization led a friend to create a business in rural South America exchanging defaced and damaged dollars for new ones. He would buy damaged dollars at a discount and replace them. The most spectacular example was a $100 bill that had been eaten by mice; the individual pieces had been recovered from the mouse droppings and sown back together. He bought this patchwork bill for $60, and it is now in the collection of the Dallas Federal Reserve.

Where trust in currency and records of ownership or income are weaker, so is the speed, efficacy and opportunity for transactions. Many developing economies have cumbersome or non-existent property registers, stunting real estate transactions. For people making their living outside of formal institutions, even something as simple as verifying earnings is a challenge. This trust problem permeates across many systems in developing countries, from lack of trust in aid distribution to lack of trust in elections.

From Gavin's book, *Frontier*:

...In Kenya, every election has been a dead heat, with 45% for one tribal grouping and 45% for another. Victory comes down to who can "steal" the remaining 10%, says Mwalimu Mati, a lawyer who runs an anti-corruption watchdog in Nairobi.

That game gets played out in the electoral commission that's meant to oversee fairness in the polling stations and declare the results. The system breaks down because the commission is itself made up of political appointees. "It's as if the players choose the referees," says Mati. "People don't trust any electoral commissions we've ever had."

For Kenyans, it's just another corruptible institution—like the police, education and transportation. Kenya ranks among the 20 worst countries for fatal road accidents partly because the driving test can be bought—and that's the way it's been for decades.

A first-time visitor to Nigeria might be struck by how much property is not for sale. Why is this noteworthy? The world over, only a small proportion of real estate is on the market for sale at any given time. What makes the situation in Nigeria remarkable is that much of the property that is not for sale is labelled as such on billboards on empty land or paint daubed on the walls of homes warning: "This house is not for sale."

Sometimes the signs read "Beware 419." This refers to Section 419 of the Nigerian Penal Code outlawing fraud. While scammers, known in Nigeria as 419ers, are renowned internationally for their expertly pitched email scams—with just enough misspelling to hook the more credulous—a popular scam back home is to sell a property you don't own, pocket the money and disappear before the new buyer encounters the real owner.

419 scams are possible because Nigeria's institutions are ineffective in securing trust in property registration. In most developed countries, an interested buyer can quickly check a national or provincial land register online to confirm the current ownership of any property. The potential buyer knows that the land register includes all of the property in the province and that the relevant agency for property registration updates the register whenever there are changes in ownership. Should the buyer go ahead with a transaction, they can also be assured that any legal dispute over title can, at least in the first instance, be decided fairly swiftly. And, for those instances where this system fails, the risk of such failure is born not by the transaction participants, but by an intermediary in the form of title insurance.

The situation is exactly the opposite in Nigeria. No integrated database of property registration exists. Some states keep a mix of electronic and paper records; other states, only paper records. If a prospective buyer wants to persist with a paper record search, she will first need to find a way to view the database. Access is limited. More importantly, the register is not comprehensive even in the biggest cities, let alone in rural areas. Should the buyer decide to go ahead with a purchase and subsequently find herself in a dispute over title, she should expect to wait at least three years for first judgment and further years for any subsequent appeals. Title insurance is made practically impossible because there is not enough infrastructure or data to build an effective actuary table, even for the most determined buyer.

The World Bank Doing Business project has constructed an index to measure the quality of property registration institutions globally. Out of a maximum score of 30, Nigeria's range from 9 in Lagos State to 4.5 in Kano State, with the variation dependent on the degree of digitization of the process. Sub-Saharan Africa's major economies—with Kenya at 15, South Africa at

15.5—trail middle-income economies, such as Malaysia (26.5) and China (24), and developed economies like the UK (26), or Japan (25.5).[1] That said, African countries are not alone in scoring poorly. Notable laggards elsewhere in the world include Greece (4.5), Venezuela (5.5) and, relative to developed nation peers, the US (17.6) (Fig. 2.1).[2]

The example of weak property registration in Nigeria exposes inadequacies in another critical infrastructure to support trust—the legal system. In developed economies, legal precedent serves as a distributed system for enforcing norms of trust. Though centralized in the creation of law through legislative bodies, the administration of law and the mechanism through which it interfaces with reality is carried out by a distributed network of judges and juries. Centuries of deliberation are documented in the form of legal opinions and judgements, providing a blueprint for how trust is to be enforced.

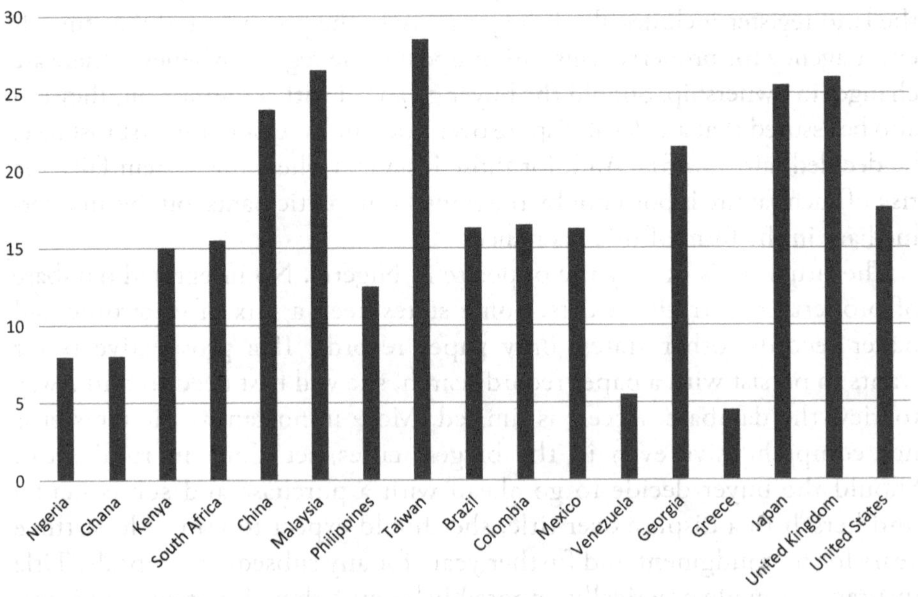

Fig. 2.1 Index measuring the quality of property registration institutions globally. Source: The World Bank Doing Business project

[1] It should be noted that Rwanda, which has focused for many years on improving its business environment, scores 28.5, tying for best in the world with the Netherlands, Taiwan, Singapore and Lithuania.

[2] https://www.doingbusiness.org/en/data/exploretopics/registering-property.

One further key area that the World Bank's Doing Business project benchmarks is the ease of enforcing contracts. While there are plenty of exceptions, developing economies overall perform relatively poorly. Even leaving aside potential issues of fairness and corruption, one of the most important aspects for a company enforcing a contract is how long the legal process will take. If the process drags on, then the claimant may go bust long before they receive the benefits of contract enforcement. Similarly, if the cost of enforcing the contract is too high relative to the size of the claim, a claimant might simply not bother.

To put this in perspective, if we look at the high-income members of the Organisation for Economic Co-operation and Development (OECD), it takes an average 590 days to enforce a contract (though with Greece as a notable laggard at 1711 days) and at a cost of 21.5% of the contract value. In sub-Saharan Africa the time is not much longer at 655 days, but the cost doubles to 41.6% of the contract value. By contrast, in both South Asia and Latin America, the increase in cost is less substantial, at around 30%, but companies must cope with much more drawn out timelines of 1100 days for Latin America. Such situations can be truly debilitating for commerce and businesses (Fig. 2.2).[3]

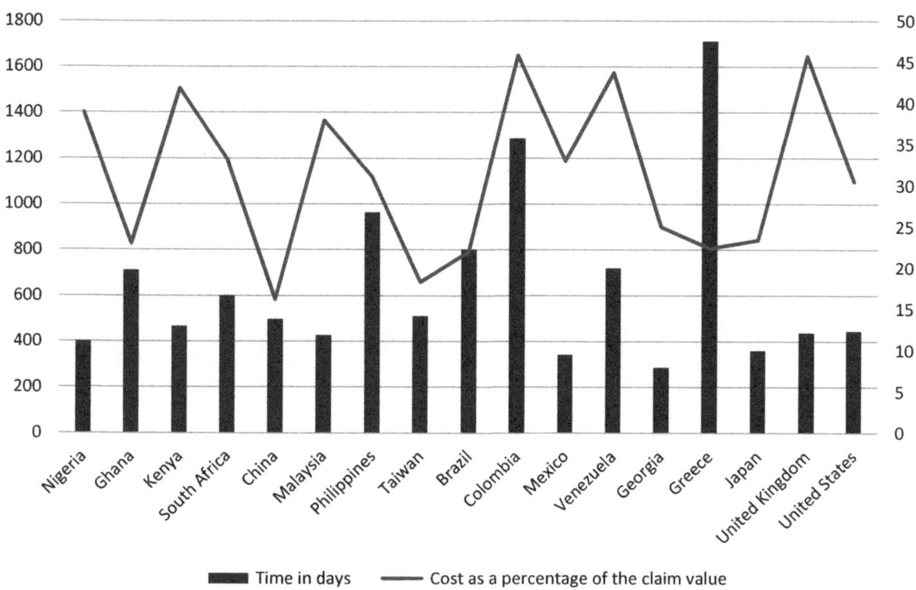

Fig. 2.2 Contract enforcement: days to enforce and cost of enforcement as a percentage of contract value. Source: The World Bank Doing Business project

[3] https://www.doingbusiness.org/en/data/exploretopics/enforcing-contracts.

Could blockchain-based systems augment or replace some of the weak or non-existent institutions of trust in developing countries? For property registration as with digital identity and contracts, potential applications are starting to take hold. However, as we will explore further, while blockchains can provide some elements of the solution, the achilles heel lies in creating a set of trusted procedures to make sure that the data recorded in these new systems is itself reliable.

3

What Does Blockchain Solve?

Blockchain technology has been around for over a decade yet most of the world is only just beginning to understand the ramifications, opportunities and dangers of the concepts unleashed. From digital identity to the use of cryptocurrencies, blockchain goes to the heart of the role of government and companies, and our place in human society and the economy.

"My word is my bond," the motto of the London Stock Exchange, is widely recognized and purported to be the moral underpinning of a banker's relationship with her clients. Our financial system has always required us to "trust" in third-party institutions. The Global Financial Crisis that began in 2007 called many to question whether this trust was well founded.

Blockchain technology at its heart is a tool for interaction between people and entities. Mathematics and computer code form the mechanism through which information can be autonomously authenticated. It provides the particpants with confidence that the information in a transaction is beyond the influence of any one person or entity. When corrupted, the data breach is there for all to see. With this level of transparency and traceability, there is no longer a need to know a counterparty, nor to involve any mutually trusted institution. Trust is in the code that underlies the system.

The ability to verify that information is true is the foundation on which transactions in the modern economy are built. The traditional expectation is that third-party intermediaries—government agencies, banks, audit firms and the like—provide verification and assurance to transacting parties. And this is where the system breaks down, particularly in developing economies. For transactions to be worthwhile to the third parties, they must be scalable to extract value. That becomes particularly difficult when serving poorer rural

P. Domjan et al., *Chain Reaction*, https://doi.org/10.1007/978-3-030-51784-7_3

communities. The present system has been good enough until now in the developed world. Blockchain is showing that a better mechanism for trust may exist for the developing world at least.

Risk Tolerance and Risk Culture: Are We Built for Blockchain?

But while blockchain technology might help to reduce one set of risks by allowing transactions to be verified more easily, other new and different risk characteristics must first be understood. Take the original application of blockchain: Bitcoin. The holder of the private key to a Bitcoin wallet controls the wallet. There is no "forgot password" or "reset my pin" option. If you lose control over your Bitcoin wallet, you lose your bitcoin.

Wall Street used to function in much the same way. In the late nineteenth and early twentieth centuries as stock markets were emerging, ownership was proven by physical share certificates. Transactions were consummated by physically delivering these certificates between counterparties. This soon became cumbersome, and so runners were hired to ferry certificates from one party to the other, first on foot, then by bicycle. Given the physicality of this system, transactions in equities became concentrated in certain cities—most notably, New York. With growth of the stock market, this system too ultimately became too cumbersome, and so the US system we use today emerged, whereby all stock certificates are owned by one little-known entity. Cede & Co and its parent, the Depository Trust and Clearing Corporation (DTCC), are entrusted to maintain an electronic ledger of who owns which stocks, providing efficiency to the system and negating the need for physical transfer.

Many people are startled to learn that the stock they think they "own" is in fact not even held in their name. This has led to issues where more claims exist on shares than the actual shares in circulation.[1] When Dole Foods was taken private in 2013, valid claims of existing stock exceeded the actual shares available by 33%.[2]

Now, once again, investors are exploring new systems to manage asset ownership. This is no easy task given differing bylaws, compliance

---

[1] Eha, Brian Patrick. 2016. You Don't Really Own Your Securities: Can Blockchain Fix That? *American Banker*, 27 July. https://www.americanbanker.com/news/you-dont-really-own-your-securities-can-blockchains-fix-that. Accessed 12 February 2019.

[2] Levine, Matt. 2017. Dole Foods Had Too Many Shares. *Bloomberg*, 17 February. https://www.bloomberg.com/opinion/articles/2017-02-17/dole-food-had-too-many-shares. Accessed 22 February 2019.

requirements, client expectations and our evolving comprehension of how to secure assets.

Ownership of an asset on a blockchain works through a system of records being verified and stored cryptographically to reduce certain risks—such as confiscation, censorship or exposure to third-party solvency. It also comprehensively assigns both liability and sovereignty to the transaction counterparties. The change in risk culture required is explicit. With the transaction flow being defined by code and consensus algorithms rather than traditional intermediaries and regulations, the institutional liability arrangements on which we have relied for decades are no longer compatible. This requires total adjustment in our understanding of risk.

This shift in attitude to risk comes easier for those used to operating in places normally perceived as inherently riskier and by those less encumbered by an existing infrastructure of risk control. While eliminating risk is clearly impossible, this nevertheless continues to be a common regulatory and organizational objective in the developed world. By contrast, culture in developing countries accepts the inevitability of a certain degree of risk.

To an extent Covid-19 levelled the playing field when it comes to acceptance of risk. And there is a valid argument that rather than seeking to minimize risk, humans naturally adjust their behavior to optimize the outcomes for given level of risk. This is the theory of risk homeostasis, which originated in research seeking to understand why road traffic fatalities didn't seem to fall as cars became safer. Researchers found that motorists have a particular level of risk that they are willing to tolerate rather than a particular outcome that they are seeking to achieve with minimum required risk. When cars become safer, motorists compensate by taking greater risks on the road, allowing them to optimize the outcome of their driving within their risk envelope.[3] For example, by driving faster in a safer car, a driver experiences the same risk as they would driving slower in a less safe car, but with the added benefit of arriving sooner or having a more thrilling journey. Although risk and protection have many more layers in any large and complex organization, individual

[3] For an overview of the theory of risk homeostasis, see: Wilde, G.J.S. 1998. Risk Homeostasis Theory: An Overview. *Injury Prevention*, 4.

behavior and risk appetite still play a major role.[4] The dynamics of homeostasis are self-evident among professional risk takers, such as investors or insurers.[5]

This approach to risk has significant implications for the use of blockchain. A new technology that simplifies verification, and thereby reduces risk, is more likely to be utilized. By reducing the risk of one component of a transaction (verification), this allows counterparties to tolerate greater risk in other aspects of a transaction, such as self-sovereignty—thereby increasing economic activity.

Verification Beats Trust

Borrowing from a phrase popularized by Ronald Reagan with reference to Cold War nuclear arms deals, the motto of Bitcoiners and others in the blockchain community is "Don't trust, verify."

Based on this approach, many evangelists use the word "trustless" to describe emerging blockchain systems. This is inaccurate. Blockchain technology does not remove the need for a trusted intermediary between counterparties. Rather, the blockchain itself becomes the trusted intermediary, replacing a third-party institution with technology.

In this sense, blockchain itself isn't a solution to the trust problem; it is a new layer that provides a different approach to security. It benefits users by being a more scalable, more transparent model for transactions and records, with the potential to support many different applications.

Some have likened the emerging technology to the rise of the World Wide Web. But rather than a new internet, it is more akin to the underlying tech stack that enabled the internet to happen. It was the technology of HTTP and TCP/IP protocol, and the ARPANET network, that provided a new infrastructure for communication, enabling an array of applications, from blogs and webmail to VOIP and video streaming, Uber and WeChat. What HTTP, TCP/IP and ARPANET did for communications, blockchain is doing for trust in transactions.

It takes time before mature applications develop to take advantage of new technology. ARPANET, the network that became the internet, was first established in 1969. The first email was sent across the ARPANET network in

[4] Reason, J. 2016. *Managing the Risks of Organizational Accidents*. Routledge.

[5] Wargo, D.T., N.A. Baglini, and K.A. Nelson. 2010. The New Millennium's First Global Financial Crisis: The Neuroeconomics of Greed, Self-Interest, Deception, False Trust, Overconfidence and Risk Perception. Neuroeconomics and the Firm, 78–98.

1971. It took another 18 years for the World Wide Web to arrive. Even with the introduction of the World Wide Web in 1989, it was another 20 years before the most commonly used applications such as Uber and WeChat emerged.

These apps are only possible because of the innovation layer on top of established technologies.[6] Looking at the apparent pace of digital innovation today, it's easy to forget that the internet as it exists stands on the shoulders of giants—innovators from as far back as the 1960s that laid the foundation of what has become a mature ecosystem.

To understand what this means, consider building a new website 15 years ago versus today. The modern web developer can implement Google-quality search, chat or world-class visualizations with a few lines of code using libraries and other off-the-shelf services. Even non-developers can build quality digital experiences, and professionals can create advanced e-commerce, analytics and search functionality in a matter of minutes. Fifteen years ago, almost anything digital required in-house development with thousands of lines of code.[7]

So where are we in the evolution of blockchain? When will we see its results? By analogy to development of the internet, we are closer to 2005 than 1969. Use cases are emerging that could fundamentally shake our world—and many of these applications begin in developing countries. In fact, blockchains can, and will, interact with all of the internet-enabled tech or smart tech: internet of things, machine learning, artificial intelligence, ubiquitous connectivity. These technologies are really about creating systems that do things better than we humans can—whether faster, more safely or for less money. Blockchains could become the transactional lifeblood that enables these technologies to become more effective.

Throughout this book, we illustrate the potential and challenges through real-life case studies of blockchains currently in progress in developing countries, and through interviews for perspective from those leading the projects. While some of the detail discussed might appear complex, it is the overall concepts, ideas and possibilities that are key to understanding the potential of blockchain.

[6] Greg Satell and Peter Hinssen discuss the differing pace of fundamental and application layer innovation in "The End of the Digital Revolution," an episode of the London Business School Review podcast: https://soundcloud.com/londonbusinessschool/the-end-of-the-digital-revolution-peter-hinssen.

[7] To add further perspective, in 1993 when Paul worked on developing an early shopping website just figuring out how to get the site to remember what the person wanted to buy from the beginning to end of the transaction was a challenge.

Case Study: Syria—War Crimes—Hala Systems

What they did: During the decade-long Syrian civil war that has killed 500,000 people, Hala Systems has been applying an early warning system for detecting and reporting attacks to not only help save lives but additionally collate immutable evidence as a tool to hold regimes to account at the International Criminal Court (ICC).

How it works: For every airstrike or ground offensive, there is a multitude of data generated by humans and machines—from satellite images to hospital admittance—that proves when, where and how an attack occurred. Hala Systems' team takes each piece of information, converts it through an algorithm into a unique series of 64 numbers and letters, and enters this as a "block." The next block has in its data a hash from the previous block, creating the "chain." Should someone from Hala Systems or anywhere else try to change one block of evidence, every block would be altered, and the manipulated report would be rendered inadmissible. If the report remains identical to the original, it becomes admissible evidence.

How it's going: After running a live pilot with the company ConsenSys using the Ethereum blockchain, Hala Systems has been stress testing for scenarios such as an internet of things (IoT) device becoming corrupted, or for malicious actors to discover the identity of individuals in Hala's network of reporters. Hala Systems is now working out options and partners to move the project forward.

Verdict: The fact that information is logged on a blockchain and is difficult to change doesn't make the information true. The risk is that falsified records or doctored photographs enter the blockchain. The challenge, therefore, is to ensure that the machines and humans collecting the evidence are cross-correlated to check for inconsistencies and weed out false indicators. With that said, it is hard to think of a worthier cause for blockchain. Presidents and warlords repeatedly slip from ICC prosecutors after years of costly investigation because of witness intimidation and evidence tampering. Immutable evidence gathering could ultimately help mitigate future conflicts.

Practitioner Perspective: COVID Testing

Genevieve Leveille, CEO of OTT8 Group, a company using blockchain to authenticate coronavirus testing kits

1. **What's the big idea behind test kit verification?**

Verifiable tracing of the supply chain adds transparency, uniformity and trust. When the manufacturer or purchaser of a Covid-19 test kit is able to track her product, there is an inherent trust built between the two ends of the chain. This transparency leads to better relationships, secure purchasing and, in the case of medical tests and therapeutic treatments, more certainty around efficacy.

2. **Why is it important in an emerging markets context?**

In the case of Covid test kits, the volume manufacturers are based in China; this is in fact true of many medical tests and drugs. Quality controls in China have been called into question in the past (recall the 2008 baby milk scandal), to the detriment of bona fide manufacturers. We have built the O8 supply chain management ecosystem to provide a low-cost mechanism through which manufacturers can demonstrate in a verifiable way that their product has been manufactured and delivered according to certain specified standards.

3. **How does it all work?**

In the wake of the Covid-19 pandemic, "kits" designed to test for the presence of a current infection and/or antibodies from a previous infection have played an important role in identifying cases, providing early stage treatment and preventing further spread, and therefore have been critical to public health strategy.

Given the importance of test kits, it follows that the efficacy of the kits should be monitored and the manufacturers and service providers should be held accountable. Early in the pandemic, it appears there were faulty and unreliable kits distributed across the world.

The O8 ecosystem is designed to provide a verifiable supply chain utilizing secured IoT devices to capture supply chain data in real time, including location and ambient conditions; enterprise blockchain (Corda R3) for the recording and verification of the supply chain data; certification of manufacturers, attesting to test kit efficacy and quality; and a Covid-19 immunity passport with a verified and GDPR compliant identity certificate.

4. **Who are the influencers in this field?**

Most important are the regulatory boards and governments who define the rules and regulations to be adhered to throughout the value chain, along with the findings and recommendations of the World Health Organization.

5. **What has been achieved so far in this area?**

Distributed ledger technology (DLT) has been in limited use in the healthcare supply chain. The solutions are thus far very rudimentary. The US Food and Drug Administration has been running a number of proof of concept trials to support the Drug Supply Chain Security Act requirements, which mandate an interoperable confidential change of ownership system within the pharmaceutical supply chain. There does not exist as of today a solution that connects the various actors in the value chain.

6. **What still needs to be done?**

There is a clear need for effective identification and assurance of the supply chain by ensuring traceability from reagent to patient, and an opportunity to efficiently meet regulatory requirements, validation of product safety and transportation conditions, mapping of geographic location and connecting various actors in the supply chain.

DLT solutions would also allow for disintermediation, thus having a cost-reducing impact on supply chain transactions.[8] The IoT and AI would provide reliable information to consumers about the provenance and authentic product history, by utilizing scannable QR codes or near-field communication (NFC) tags on packaging.

7. **Given the enormity of the challenge, what is your approach through 08?**

By integrating DLT and AI and other disruptive technologies in an orchestrated approach, we will achieve a full cycle of transparency and trust throughout the value chain.

8. **What is the biggest challenge to mainstream acceptance?**

Blockchain technology has seen a lot of success around cryptocurrencies; however, misuse of that capital creation has also caused a misunderstanding about the opportunities that the technology brings to bear. Insufficient resources make most blockchain projects expensive propositions. Furthermore, because there is a lack of standards, no one knows what good is, but we see a lot of what bad is. This lack of knowledge demands education at the level of individuals and most importantly at the level of regulators.

[8] https://www.tandfonline.com/doi/full/10.1080/00207543.2019.1657247.

9. **What is the biggest danger in terms of something going badly wrong in this space?**

The greatest threat would be an unforeseen global pandemic coupled with a scenario where everything grinds to a halt—where there is a major power outage, for example. You would have data centers but no electricity; computers with no ability to compute.

10. **Where do you see tracing in five years' time?**

Blockchain will become ubiquitous. It will be used for everything from healthcare and farming, to regulations and supply chain management. It has potential to be used to track where companies are sourcing their materials from and keep them in line with laws and regulations.

4

Who Really Controls Blockchain?

Understanding how blockchains work begins with an appreciation of the first: Bitcoin.

The market for bitcoin and other cryptocurrencies is nothing if not volatile—and with good reason given its nascent and evolutionary nature (Fig. 4.1).

Even the language used to describe blockchains, and the cryptocurrencies and tokens that reside within them, is in flux. All of the words used, no matter how common, fall short in some manner when compared to how they are used in every day vernacular. So fundamental are the changes created by blockchain that our lexicon needs to evolve beyond established vocabulary.

Take cryptocurrencies. Are they even "currencies"? Traditional fiat currencies are issued by central banks. Governments guarantee that they will be accepted as "legal tender" for transactions and payment of taxes. These qualities are clearly not applicable to bitcoin or any other cryptocurrency. Yet, from Argentina to Zimbabwe, we have seen multiple examples of how confidence of these traits in a fiat currency can collapse as soon as trust in the government and institutional framework behind the monetary system crumbles.

Exactly "how" a cryptocurrency derives its value is also debatable. Here's our own discussion about the value of bitcoin:

Paul: Bitcoin is valuable for much the same reason that amber and lapis lazuli are valuable—because someone else is willing to value it. It's not because of any intrinsic usefulness. Commodities like gold and oil have similar dynamics, except that they have more obvious intrinsic usefulness. Even financial assets have many of the same properties.

P. Domjan et al., *Chain Reaction*, https://doi.org/10.1007/978-3-030-51784-7_4

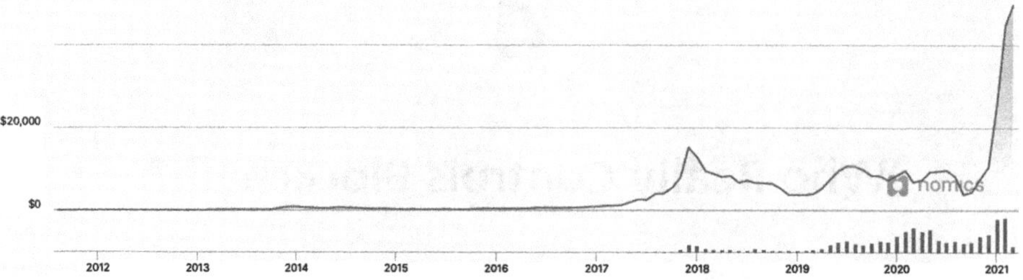

Fig. 4.1 Bitcoin price (in USD). Source: Nomics

Brandon: I'd argue that the value of bitcoin is intrinsic. It is valuable because of the time, money and other resources that are spent to operate the network. There are thousands investing their software development expertise, computer hardware, energy resources and other assets to ensure the Bitcoin network operates in the way it is designed to.

John: You're both partially right. The value of Bitcoin is a function both of its utility and its network security. It is more complex than a simple supply versus demand relationship. Demand relates to the exchange rate of fiat currency vs. bitcoin. But it is the computing power used to sustain the system—the proof of work—that in turn provides security. The greater the security, the greater the demand for Bitcoin and the greater are the rewards for those providing the security, which in turn brings more capital and more computing power. It's a virtuous circle, that also works in reverse if demand falls or security degrades.

Gavin: This is true—for now. But it might not be true tomorrow. The concept of creating value through computer power, or proof of work, is viewed by many as unsustainable—both from the perspective of carbon emissions through all of the electricity demanded, and in terms of the slow pace of transactions. Instead of the current system, some advocate moving towards "proof of stake," in which a network of validators deposit money and use it as collateral to vouch for a block. Whereas "proof of work" assigns value based on computer work, under "proof of stake" the value lies in the underlying collateral in a similar way to an asset-backed bond. It must be said, momentum for this is coming more from the Ethereum than the Bitcoin community.

Bitcoin Versus bitcoin

There are two concepts that share the same word. We use the capitalized "Bitcoin" to refer to the overall system or blockchain. We use "bitcoin" with a lowercase "b" for the cryptocurrency, coin or token that is used as a means to measure or convey the value transferred with each transaction. This is the typical nomenclature throughout the crypto realm (e.g. "Ethereum" has "ether").

At the time of publishing, around 18.6 million bitcoins had been mined.[1] The predetermined ceiling is 21 million. Currently, new bitcoins are released into the network at a rate of around 900 per day. The rate at which new bitcoins are released into the blockchain halves every few years or, more specifically, after every 210,000 blocks – or sets of transactions added to the blockchain. The most recent halving took place in May 2020.

How it all works is related to four primary roles, each with their own set of incentives to participate:

1. Users: The people or entities that engage in a transaction of bitcoin. The only requirement is an internet connection. No third party is able to directly affect the transaction once initiated and executed.

2. Node operators: When a user sends a bitcoin to another user, a transaction is created. This transaction is then submitted, or broadcast, via the internet to over a thousand copies of the Bitcoin blockchain software, or Bitcoin nodes. Each node operator "hears" this transaction, and places it among the pool of received but not yet confirmed transactions, called a mempool. Crucially, operators can also submit their own transactions to the network. They are incentivized to listen for other users' transactions in order to get direct, real-time access to the exact state of the Bitcoin blockchain—including confirmed and unconfirmed transactions. Only these operators know exactly what transactions have been validated at a particular point in time. While it is possible for others to view the current state of transactions through various tools, these views are not nearly as trustable because the data will lag the true current state of the blockchain and could have been altered. In this way, when operators choose to engage in their own transaction, they can have 100% certainty that their

[1] https://www.coinmarketcap.com.

transaction is legitimate as they control one of the nodes. They can ensure that the software is current, the data is up-to-date, and the stream of transactions are validated. Without this direct visibility, the risk for errors, delays or outright fraud is greater. Although most users are comfortable with waiting for confirmation by the network, those transacting at high volumes are less willing to wait or take on this additional risk. Those managing other peoples' bitcoin or engaging in large transactions require the reliability and security of running their own node.

3. Developers: The people who make changes to the code that underlies Bitcoin.

The rhetoric around Bitcoin uses words like "trustless" and "decentralized" in an attempt to describe management and control of the system. The reality is that people do control the system. Bitcoin developers are the key actors—tasked with improving and iterating the underlying code of the system. The people involved with the development of Bitcoin Core, so far the dominant code base used for Bitcoin, is a small cabal of individuals, some merely interested in supporting the system, others funded by either wealth generated from Bitcoin's rise in value or employed by companies with interests in Bitcoin's progress. To date, nearly 700 people have contributed at least some code to the existing Bitcoin Core codebase. Thousands more have tried but been denied the opportunity to contribute.[2]

Code contribution begins by a contributor proposing a change. The community has a well-defined set of specifications. Each change must be peer reviewed, whereby other contributors review the code to check its quality. Contributors with more code already included have greater clout to help determine which changes are admitted and which are not.

An even tighter circle has credentials to merge the proposed code to the master codeset. Currently a handful of individuals have been granted such access. Who are these individuals and how are they chosen? According to Jameson Lopp's discussion in December 2018 titled, "Who Controls Bitcoin Core," the Bitcoin Core keys were registered to Wladimir J. van der Laan, Pieter Wuille, Jonas Schnelli, Marco Falke and Samuel Dobson.

Does this mean that Bitcoin users are entrusting these five people to run the blockchain? Not quite. Whoever owns the keys arguably does "control" Bitcoin. However, the pressure for this inner core of super-developers is whether or not the community ends up adopting the code delivered. Users

[2] https://github.com/bitcoin/bitcoin.

can choose not to update their copy of the Bitcoin code to the latest version, or they could choose a different version altogether. Such conflicts are often managed but sometimes bubble into all out wars, with detractors moving to their own version of Bitcoin. To date, there are dozens of blockchains that originated with Bitcoin Core but have subsequently forked off into their own community, complete with their own codebase and governance system. None have managed to near the market value of the Bitcoin Core system. Yet.

This pressure of being replaced prods the contributors to meet the needs and interests of the community. Those that disagree can break off easily and try to bring the community (and the market) with them. So far, the incentive structure has allowed Bitcoin Core to iterate and evolve, albeit slowly, and the market continues to follow.[3]

4. Miners: The people or entities that run specialized computers or in some cases vast pools of hundreds or thousands of computers, tasked with appending new blocks to the chain, validating blocks in the chain and securing the overall network. Mining is designed as a race, using a process known as proof-of-work where the winner is rewarded with a predetermined number of bitcoins and the transaction fees on the newly formed block, known as the block reward.

As of May 2020, the newly minted bitcoins included in the block reward was halved from 12.5 to 6.25 bitcoins. As previously mentioned, this halving, as it is known, occurs every 210,000 blocks or roughly every four years as dictated by the protocol. There will only ever be 21 million bitcoins, once the last satoshi (fraction of a bitcoin) has been minted sometime around the year 2140. From then on, miners' compensation will consist solely of transaction fees. These vary with each block, determined by demand for transactions and the number of transactions awaiting inclusion in a new block.

Integral to the proof-of-work mechanism is the concept of "hashing." A hash function takes a set of data and creates a unique string of characters and numbers, known as a "hash." The hashing used by the Bitcoin protocol is a one-way function where the resulting hash cannot be reversed to reveal the inputs. Any data can be hashed and any change to the source (even one pixel of a digital image) will produce a different hash, making the hash a convenient way of checking whether known inputs have been altered.

---

[3] A more detailed discussion of who controls Bitcoin Core can be found here: https://blog.lopp.net/who-controls-bitcoin-core-/.

SHA256("Hello World") =	SHA256("Hello Worl") =
a591a6d40bf4204	12fec4c65dd4455c
04a011733cfb7b19	48aff8977a7cd8cc
0d62c65bf0bcda32b	b97539ad4cd7c37f
57b277d9ad9f146e	13cf71ba8bee9a98

Fig. 4.2 Secure Hashing Algorithm 256 (SHA256) in practice: the hash of "Hello World" vs. the hash of "Hello Worl"

The hash function used in the Bitcoin system is known as SHA-256. It produces a fixed length output of 64 numbers and letters in hexadecimal format (Fig. 4.2).

To see SHA-256 working in practice, access one of the many online SHA-256 calculators. Type this phrase: "the quick brown fox jumped over the lazy dog." You will see that the SHA-256 hash of that phrase is: 20c1892df4e-665666558289367ae1682d1f93bc5be4049627492cdb5a42635e4.

Now, change the phrase to: "the quick *red* fox jumped over the lazy dog." You will see that the hash has changed. Revert to the original phrase and the original hexadecimal code returns.

In the Bitcoin protocol, the proof-of-work process begins with the miner using a prescribed algorithm to generate a random "number only used once," or nonce for short. To "win" the race to append the new block, the miner must compute a hash that begins with at least the same number of zeros that has been predetermined by the protocol, known as the target. Each miner will produce millions of attempts in an effort to be the first to figure out a hash below the target, and win the block race. Think of it as computers repeatedly pushing a button. Each push of the button kicks off a defined set of procedures to randomly generate the number. Ultimately, the effect is to eat processing power and energy from the miner's system. Once a low enough nonce has been generated, that nonce is then combined with the hash of the current block, and hashed with the previous block, thereby creating the next "block" of confirmed transactions on the Bitcoin blockchain.

The system aims to keep block creation steady at around one block every 10 minutes. If a rise in the number of miners competing increases their collective work, or "hash power," or the number of submissions per second increases, known as the "hash rate," then the system will make a "difficulty adjustment," adding more zeros to make the target harder, or decreasing the number to make it easier. This calibration occurs every 2016 blocks or roughly every two weeks.

Once a winner has been established, that miner will append this new "block" of transactions to the Bitcoin blockchain. Other miners will then test the legitimacy of the new block by checking the propagated hash against other known data points. This process is referred to as "consensus." It enables thousands of miners to come to agreement every 10 minutes as to the current, validated state of the network. The fact that this can happen at such scale and in this short period among a network of unknown computers is the crux of the innovation Bitcoin has unleashed.

The system for validating and securing blocks is deliberately energy intensive. This is core to the entire incentive structure of Bitcoin, determining how value is transferred from parties in the transaction to operators to miners, even in warding off attackers and speculators. The costly validation process is also at the heart of how the system itself generates value. Otherwise it becomes cheap enough for malicious actors to subvert the system. The simplest, most ubiquitous artifact of value is energy.

At certain points in its history, mining bitcoin at the global average cost per kilowatt hour of energy would not have been profitable.[4] One positive consequence of this dynamic is that many large-scale efforts to mine bitcoin are funnelling their spend on cheaper forms of electricity, namely renewables. The most lucrative mining operations are located near large-scale hydro, wind or other renewable generation facilities, supporting more research and investment in such technologies.

Other coins, notably Ethereum, are much more energy efficient, and their efficiency could improve further as proof-of-work systems are challenged by less energy-intensive validation and security mechanisms, such as proof-of-stake, proof-of-space or other structures.

The security of Bitcoin derives from the difficulty of faking it. While "hacking" the cryptography would allow a miner to solve the function faster, this would present two new challenges. The first is that the winner of each block reward is public knowledge to all participants so, if one miner consistently wins, you can bet hundreds of others will dig in to understand why. Second, the difficulty of the hashing function to be solved is variable. The Bitcoin system is designed to automatically increase or reduce the level of complexity, depending primarily on the speed at which miners are able to solve the hash function. By hacking the system, a miner might speed up the process, causing

[4] Even within the US, energy costs vary widely, from US$0.10 per kilowatt hour in the northern Midwest to over US$0.27 per kilowatt hour in Alaska and Hawaii; https://www.eia.gov/electricity/monthly/epm_table_grapher.php?t=epmt_5_6_a. Accessed 12 April 2019.

Fig. 4.3 Antminer S9 13.5 TH/S Bitcoin Miner

the system to make subsequent functions more difficult. The complexity of the hashing function has increased over the years as computers become more and more sophisticated.

When Bitcoin was first released in 2009, miners needed nothing more than a laptop and internet connection. Eventually, computers with more advanced graphics processing units (GPUs) created an advantage over those that didn't, tilting block rewards in their favor. More recently, application-specific integrated circuits (ASICs) have been developed to further improve the probability of winning the Bitcoin block rewards (Fig.4.3).

Custom development of integrated circuits is nothing new. This is how our cell phones have become smaller, yet more powerful. However, squeezing such efficiencies out of the technology takes time and resources. Research and development for new ASICs can take years and cost millions of dollars. The first mover for developing Bitcoin ASICs took a risk, and once they began mining using the new technology, their bet was public for all to see, stoking fast followers to develop their own. Today, Bitcoin can only be successfully mined using one of several ASIC miners currently on the market.

Miners are not known to brag about their latest and greatest gear, so major improvements in hardware technology are usually only understood by observing changes in the distribution of block rewards. With each new technology advantage discovered, the cost to compete in both hardware and power required goes up.

A key feature of this incentive structure is that it allows for the system to be permissionless, for the most part—no gatekeepers exist to determine who can and cannot participate as a user, operator or miner. The system is secure enough and the rules defined in such a manner that anyone can choose to participate as a user, node operator or miner. Anyone can access the system simply by downloading the software.

Valuing Bitcoin

Ever-decreasing supply supports the case for value in Bitcoin, especially when compared with increased printing of the US dollar and other fiat currencies for post-Covid stimulus packages. But this mechanism has also led to hoarding of bitcoin by speculators. While many users have forgotten their private key, disabling access to their bitcoin, others keep them securely, unused but not forgotten.[5]

As the price of bitcoin has risen, so too has the amount of "stagnant" bitcoin—bitcoin that hasn't recently been transferred from one wallet to another in a transaction (Fig. 4.4).[6]

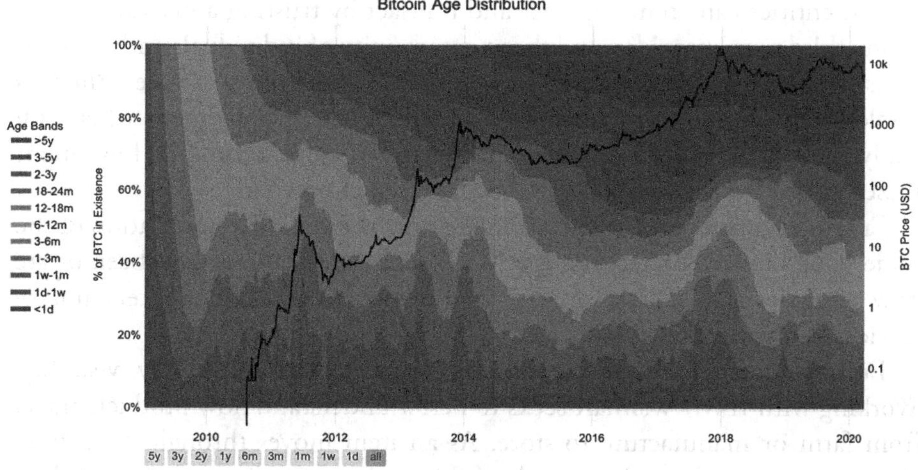

Fig. 4.4 Time since each bitcoin was last transacted. Source: Unchained Capital

[5] One of the more famous stories of lost bitcoin is that of James Howells. He lost 7500 bitcoin (now worth over US$ 200 million) when he threw away the hard drive he used to mine bitcoin back in 2009: https://www.theguardian.com/technology/2013/nov/27/hard-drive-bitcoin-landfill-site.

[6] One of the more notable analyses of circulating supply of bitcoin was done by Dhruv Bansal of Unchained Capital: https://blog.unchained-capital.com/bitcoin-data-science-pt-1-hodl-waves-7f3501d53f63.

While demand has risen much faster than additional bitcoin made available, any fall in demand can't be compensated with reduced supply of coins. The combined effect of stagnant bitcoin and limited supply is that relatively small changes in demand lead to outsized price moves. There is simply no mechanism, as yet at least, to allow for supply to adjust in step. Unsurprisingly, therefore, the volatility of Bitcoin prices is more akin to other assets with inelastic supply, such as oil or gold, than fiat currencies.

Another distinction from almost any other investable asset is that investment in cryptocurrencies began among retail or individual consumers. More sophisticated institutional actors are only now beginning to do the research required to understand the technology and its potential. With their entry to the market comes knowledge, sophistication and infrastructure to deliver accessibility more suited to institutions. One example is JP Morgan, the largest US bank. It recently announced the development of its own cryptocurrency: JPM Coin.[7]

Blockchain as an Infrastructure

The innovation behind Bitcoin has proven that thousands of unique individuals and entities can come together and transact by trusting a network in lieu of any third party provider, and that a community of individuals and corporations can be incentivized to support this network infrastructure. Bitcoin's implementation is rudimentary as a system. But, what happens when you apply these same concepts for other systems of value transfer? How might these systems morph or contort, or be replaced altogether?

Cryptocurrencies and crypto coins are only the very first application of the underlying blockchain technology. Many more applications have been or are now being developed, from smarter legal services to property registers, notary services and voting systems.

Take Walmart's use of blockchain to improve food supply visibility. Working with IBM, Walmart seeks to better understand how products travel from farm or manufacture to store. As an item moves through the supply chain, it can pass through upwards of thirty-plus custodians, each with their

[7]This follows years of negative comments by the bank's CEO, Jamie Dimon: "In 2017 JPMorgan CEO Jamie Dimon described bitcoin as a 'fraud,' 'stupid' and 'far too dangerous' to people who traded it." https://www.cnn.com/2019/02/14/investing/jpmorgan-jpm-coin-cryptocurrency/index.html. Accessed 8 April 2019.

own often opaque method of tracking. Walmart is creating visibility on where a given item is in its supply chain at any one time.[8]

How does tracking work on the blockchain? On a farm in eastern Uganda, yellow coffee beans are funnelled at a rate of 50 kilos per minute through a 3D scanner called a bextmachine. Through this IoT input linked to the bext360 blockchain, buyers at Denver's Coda Coffee Co. can scan a QR code showing every stop of the beans, from farm through cleaning, milling and roasting.[9] Starbucks is similarly working with Microsoft's Azure Blockchain Service to trace its coffee from farmers in Costa Rica, Colombia and Rwanda.[10]

While such innovation will doubtless provide opportunities to streamline processes, visibility in the journey also offers important safety benefits, particularly with regard to food. Today, when a contaminated food is discovered, effectively all of that food is pulled from store shelves, sometimes costing billions of dollars in lost revenue for both retailer and supplier. With better visibility, Walmart hopes to be able to better trace their food supply as needed, shifting from a "carpet bomb" approach to a scalpel. Only the actual contaminated foods will need to be removed from shelves, and identification and removal can happen in a matter of minutes to hours, versus days and weeks currently.

The type of blockchain development underway at Walmart is focused primarily on cost savings. Walmart is using its market power to implement the system; as such, the blockchain is permissioned, meaning that suppliers need to be granted access. But what if the blockchain is designed in such a way that less weight is placed on Walmart's validation process for new suppliers, and more onus is put more on the system itself? How might a more open and independent, less partial or biased system help marginalized, less advantaged suppliers? How might the rest of the world's supply chain be impacted if they could leverage the knowledge that Walmart has gained over the years in ensuring a quality supply chain?

The permissionless community that has come together to run, maintain and use the Bitcoin network is a model for many other systems that could be effective at scale. These models display some characteristics similar to corporations and governments. But unlike corporations, anyone can choose to participate. Just like governments, quality blockchain projects are intent on being a public good. Unlike governments, no one is forced to subscribe to the system.

[8] https://www.ibm.com/blockchain/solutions/food-trust.

[9] https://www.wsj.com/articles/bringing-blockchain-to-the-coffee-cup-1523797205.

[10] https://news.microsoft.com/transform/starbucks-turns-to-technology-to-brew-up-a-more-personal-connection-with-its-customers/.

Such blockchain projects that take on board not just the technology but an entire stakeholder ecosystem are certainly more complex but also offer greater potential for delivering on the full potential that these new systems' templates offer. Blockchain projects focused on developing economies provide the greatest promise as fewer legacy systems need to be replaced or subverted. New incentive systems are more likely to take root where no solution is "good enough" yet. New models of trust are more likely to be tried where existing implementations or traditional models are failing.

Tokens as Pets

Before we delve into the applications in developing countries, here is some useful terminology related to coins, tokens and use cases that commonly apply to blockchain systems and projects:

Token: A digital representation of the holder's right to access or use an asset. Anytime you hear of something being tracked or traded on a blockchain, it is in fact a token that represents something. You can't put diamonds or food or anything physical "on a blockchain"—only tokens that represent that physical good.

Utility token: Enables the owner to use a service or a physical good represented by the token.

The value of tokens and utility tokens is directly linked to the underlying service or goods, and the demand for the tokens.

To understand the demand dynamic for tokens, take a look at the surreal world of owning virtual cats on the blockchain, or Cryptokitties. Each token correlates to a specific virtual cat, with its own features, lineage and characteristics. Kitties can be "bred" when two token owners agree to mix the characteristics of a kitty they own, thereby generating a new kitty. All of this is managed by a token system designed to ensure visibility and accountability on all virtual mating or other activities. Rarer characteristics and breeds accrue value as activity on the system increases: some cost hundreds and even thousands of US dollars in fiat equivalent value at the peak of Cryptokitties craziness in 2017.

This digital cats bull run coincided with the boom in token or coin offerings, or initial coin offerings (ICOs). Tokens were presold to speculative investors who hoped the price would rocket long before the system to use the tokens was even built. Masses of utility tokens were created using the Ethereum protocol. As a result, demand for Ethereum shot up. As doubts grew about the ICO fundraising model, including concerns that regulators might take action against token issuers and promoters, the demand evaporated and prices cratered, some by more than 90%.

Security token: Represents ownership of a tradeable financial instrument or security.

Thought by some to be the killer app that will bring financial institutions into the blockchain space, security tokens remain in their infancy. The technology is designed to vastly improve the efficiency and transparency with which traditional capital instruments such as stocks and bonds can be issued, traded and managed over their lifecycle. Valuing security tokens is no different to valuing a traditional security in a modern financial market.

Asset-backed tokens: Represent ownership rights in physical things—land, buildings, cars, ships, airplanes, forests; almost anything that is privately owned could be attached to a token in this way. The innovation here relates to fractional ownership, whereby an individual could own a very small percentage of an otherwise expensive asset. Tokens can be issued and managed efficiently at scale. Tokenization advocates believe that fractional ownership will bring more capital and liquidity to assets that historically have been specialized and create opportunities for individuals to participate in markets that they otherwise would be locked out of. Anyone fancy buying a 1/100,000,000th share of a commercial airliner? Valuing these assets is, again, firmly rooted in traditional finance, where the value of a token is based on the buyer's perception of what the share of the underlying asset represented by the token is worth.

Stablecoins: Tokens backed by fiat money or traded securities issued by a national government. The idea is that these instruments can be used as "currency" with a stable or observable value within a blockchain ecosystem. Proponents of stablecoins point out that the original use case for cryptocurrencies was to create an alternative to cash and that the stablecoin design facilitates adoption of crypto as an alternative to cash by providing users with a predictable value for their coins, giving them greater confidence when transferring savings from the legacy banking system into crypto. Some are linked to "baskets" of currencies and others to commodities like gold.

Stablecoin promoters all claim to hold assets backing their token on a 1:1 basis. However, the reality is hard to establish until a liquidity crisis hits or a time of high volume selling where the underlying currency backing the stablecoin needs to be provided. There is a strong parallel here with US money market funds. These mutual funds were long lauded as zero risk as they directly hold cash or securities deemed as cash equivalents, such as very short maturity US Treasury notes. Money market funds traded at prices in line with their underlying value until they "broke the buck" during the financial turmoil of 2008—and these were funds run by large institutions and experienced professionals. Regardless, stablecoins have become a prominent feature of the crypto market since 2018 and are likely to remain relevant as large-scale projects like JP Morgan's "JPM Coin," Facebook's "Diem," WeChat Pay and others develop.

Government-sponsored e-money: It is only a matter of time before governments begin to issue e-money, also referred to as Central Bank Digital Currency. In fact, e-money already exists today in many forms, including electronic representation of the money that you think of as being in your "bank account" and the money you spend when you use your debit card. This is probably best termed bank-sponsored e-money. Like physical fiat money in circulation, government-sponsored e-money would not be backed by anything other than the fiat, or decree by government. On a blockchain, e-money might be "programmable" for the purpose of collecting taxes, for example.

Blockchain and IoT: A Cautionary Tale

Nirvana for many enthusiasts combines the meticulous record keeping of the blockchain with the internet of things, or IoT. The premise is to connect more "things" to the internet, like the appliances in your home or robots used in supply chains or tools for a farmer. Digitizing such activity should have an outsized impact in developing markets, with more to gain from leapfrogging old school mechanization.

However, IoT, with its infinite stream of potential commands emanating from coffee bean counters or shipping crates, brings one major headache: scalability. The number of transactions that can be processed at any one time is finite.

Cryptokitties, the digitally reproductive cats discussed earlier, actually brought the Ethereum network to its knees in 2018. So many kitties were being bred that it choked the Ethereum network, slowing the entire system to a crawl.

To address the scalability issue in particular for IoT use cases, enter IOTA—an open-source distributed ledger and cryptocurrency designed for Internet of Things applications. Rather than using a blockchain to drive consensus as most other projects in the space, IOTA developers are employing a different mechanism, called a directed acyclic graph, or DAG.

Whereas blockchains process transactions sequentially—the next block isn't processed until after the last block was produced—DAGs allow for consensus to be reached in parallel. This means multiple sets of transactions being confirmed at any one point in time, enabling a significantly higher throughput (Fig. 4.5).

While IOTA has sought to take DAG from theoretical to real, problems and challenges have arisen. For Bitcoin, the security of the system is premised on scaling linearly with activity. A requirement of the DAG structure is that, in order for the network to be secure, a significantly larger amount of activity is necessary compared to the level for Bitcoin.

To ensure security as the network develops, IOTA implemented a role known as the coordinator. This in effect centralizes the management and security of the network until the activity reaches the level required to operate "on its own," without central coordination.

IOTA has been plagued by major security breaches. In 2020, a breach was detected whereby tokens were being siphoned from user wallets on the network. A vulnerability was exploited in wallet software, allowing the attackers to usurp US$2.3 million in tokens before IOTA engineers shut down the coordinator, effectively closing the entire network. On the one hand, it was a

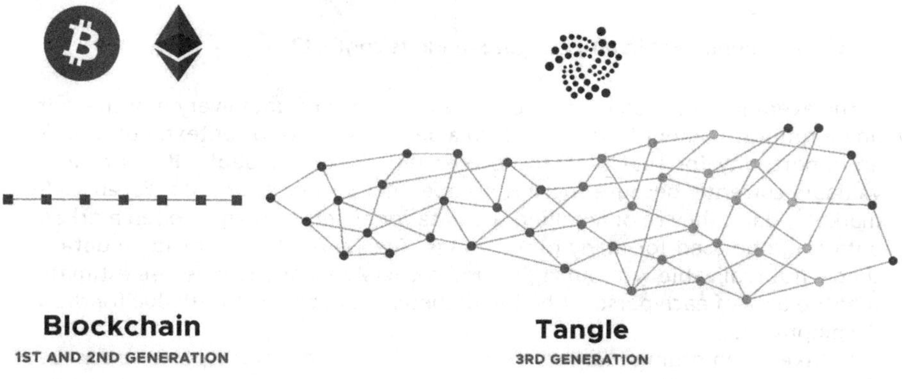

Fig. 4.5 Blockchain vs. a directed acyclic graph, or DAG. (Source: IOTA)

positive that the network was able to stop the breach. On the other, the fact that the network was able to address a breach in this manner put on full display just how centralized this network currently is, and the uphill climb to deliver on the promise of the project.

IOTA supporters have not lost faith; the market value for the project dipped only slightly even as the system remained offline. However, the challenges experienced by this project illustrate what is still to come as these experiments develop, evolve, thrive and, yes, fail.

Practitioner Perspective: Personal Data

Sean Moss-Pultz is Founder and CEO of Bitmark, a Taiwan-based company using blockchain to secure property rights for personal data

1. **What's the big idea behind control of personal data?**

If you buy into the notion that data is more valuable than oil, then you have to ask: who owns who? Are the owners the tech companies that extract our information or the individuals who embody or produce it?

Today, for the most part, people's personal data is locked into networks, such as social media platforms. The more people who join a network, the more valuable this data becomes. These locked-in networks offer us—their data producers—a little bit of control. But they ignore the most significant aspects of our rights, namely controlling our interests, including our financial interests. It's not enough.

Ultimately, rights are about control. If you have control, you can choose how you want to share your data. Determining your level of privacy is one part of that, but you also have other rights, such as the ability to move your data to another system, or to profit from your data.

2. **Why is it important in an emerging markets context?**

The average Facebook user produces $6.50 worth of data every month—not an insignificant amount, particularly in a developing world context. But there's an opportunity for that data to become much more valuable. It's not more valuable currently because there is no open marketplace for data. Facebook's market is dark: they're only selling the data for advertising. In an open market, data could be used for many other things. The value of our individual data is simply not realizable without rights and ownership. For example, we estimate that the data of each person who has diabetes could be worth $15,000 for drug development.

To take an emerging markets example, Taiwan is generally perceived to be doing well on health services post-Covid, but even here the importance of preventative healthcare is undermined. As in just about every other health information system the world over, there is no mechanism to secure people's data and their rights over their data. To resolve this problem in Taiwan, Bitmark is creating an infrastructure where those rights and that data are all in the same place: a Next-Generation Health Information Infrastructure. In our pilot program, individuals will be able to opt-in their health data to the Open Data Network. With enough participants, researchers can unlock health discoveries that will ultimately reward individuals through improved medical services. In time, the Open Data Network will support preventative health for all individuals.

3. **How does it all work?**

Before land became endowed with property rights, there was no value to it because there was no ownership or price. But with land property rights, real estate could emerge. Banks could give you mortgages without seeing your home because they knew that the property rights were clear. So, the first step is to establish rights. After that you can talk about who gets what. The moment you establish ownership rights is the moment that markets begin to function.

This extends to personal data rights. When you have clear rights, businesses will know how to use the data. They'll know what the rights are, and they'll decide what they want to pay for it. For now, there aren't clear rights because companies like Facebook take it all for themselves. And they arbitrarily determine its value based on their own usages, such as ad sales.

Experimentation can help us to create better marketplaces and exchanges. For example, we have worked to build a music marketplace for people to listen to and exchange beats. The purpose of any marketplace is to get buyers and sellers together and to create standards. The more we experiment, the better: we don't yet know what the best marketplace is.

Under the Bitmark Rights System, personal data ownership rights are recorded on the blockchain in the same way that any other asset is registered—along with records of any transfer or sharing of those assets. All the transactions are legitimized by the fact that they're recorded on a blockchain.

4. **Who are the influencers in this field?**

RadicalxChange is talking about communities pooling their data together, and getting money or generating rights from them. That's progress, but we can also have business structures. We just need to have more discussion around how businesses can turn individual ownership of data into an advantage.

Companies have demonstrated how openness can be to the advantage of their business, such as Patagonia revealing the supply chain of its clothing production. This is in contrast to other companies, such as Nike. I'm interested in a similar model for personal data, where individuals own their data and have rights to it as it's being used, while companies provide services—in the same way as you own your car and can use it, but the manufacturer can still service it.

5. **What has been achieved so far in this area?**

Almost nothing has been achieved. Data protection rules such as GDPR regulations in Europe and the CCPA in California are not having the effects intended. Instead, they've become subject to regulatory capture, in exactly the same way as regulations in the banking and pharmaceutical industries. Only big companies are able to comply because the legislation is so complex. They have all the good lawyers, and so they're locking people in. GDPR and CCPA are not addressing personal data ownership.

6. **What still needs to be done?**

There needs to be a way to build new communities that have their own data rights, which are autonomous and can be defined and enforced. Again, this is what we are looking to achieve with OurBeat. Music creators can now defend and contract their rights. Bitmark engineered these initial rights, but over time the community can change the rights to better fit their evolving needs.

7. **Given the enormity of the challenge, what is your approach through Bitmark?**

Rights are the foundation of our moral being. So we should be innovating on rights—and that's what we're doing. We are trying to show that if you experiment with different rights in different fields, you can build better communities. They generate more wealth, they're more creative, they're just better in every way.

To demonstrate this, we've engineered a few different communities, in music, in arts and in public health. They're meant to demonstrate this hypothesis, that engineering better rights can improve all of humanity. The moment we show that one or two communities really are better, people will buy in.

The role of Bitmark is to show this works, that you can build a better community if you engineer correctly.

8. **What is the biggest challenge to mainstream acceptance?**

The biggest challenge is working in a field that is dominated by large and profitable companies. In music, everything is very entrenched. In social media, Facebook is good and addictive: no one wants to get rid of it.

So we're looking into what parts of arts, humanity and science will allow us to build new communities without having so much competition. For example, public health is so broken that we can definitely build a better community. Similarly, everyone knows that the music industry is broken. That's a perfect opportunity: if everyone knows it's broken, it's time to change it.

Still, there are challenges in some of these categories as well.

Public healthcare, for example, encompasses preventative care, but this hasn't been addressed by the current system. It only deals with people who are sick, not people who want to get fitter, stronger, smarter, more productive or happier. It's very hard for technology to get in to address these issues.

9. **What is the biggest danger in terms of something going badly wrong in this space?**

The problem with the current system is that the outcomes are not as good as they could be.

For example, in the healthcare system, people don't have their own health data, so whenever they go to a hospital or clinic, they have to do all the tests again. It's a waste of resources.

Meanwhile, doing research on healthcare requires the whole data set, but the data is not in one place: it's incomplete. So researchers and doctors are not getting full information for development or diagnosis.

Of course if we did have this data all in one place, the question would be: how do you keep it safe? That's a big danger, especially for sensitive medical data.

Nonetheless, if you don't share your data, it's a missed opportunity.

10. **Where do you see personal data control in 5 years' time?**

I'm very optimistic. Within five years, personal data will be controlled by the individual.

5

Making Money

Few people living in a developed economy need cryptocurrencies to successfully go about their daily lives. Existing payments systems are faster, cheaper and much easier to use than even the most innovative cryptocurrency at this stage. Central banks exist to ensure currency stability; cryptocurrencies enjoy no such luxury. Deposit insurance schemes keep bank deposits safe. Foreign currency is readily available to facilitate international trade and tourism. People don't tend to worry about their money being trapped in the country or losing its value. Even handling physical currency is typically less risky in developed economies, given lower average crime rates. People mostly can take for granted that their currencies will fulfil all three core roles.

1. *Means of exchange*: Currencies allow us to trade without having to barter. If I have a bicycle to sell and want to buy a sandwich, I don't need to look for a sandwich seller who needs a bicycle. I can exchange my bicycle for currency, confident that I can use that currency to buy a sandwich.
2. *Store of value*: Not only do I not need to find a sandwich seller who needs a bicycle but having sold my bicycle I can save the proceeds to fund future consumption, confident that the currency that I received for my bicycle will have a similar value in the future.
3. *Unit of account*: As a bicycle seller who wants a sandwich, I don't need to work out the number of sandwiches that are worth one bicycle—I just need to know how many dollars, euros or yen a bicycle and a sandwich are worth. As a sandwich seller, I can easily work out how many sandwiches I need to sell and at what price to cover the costs of ingredients, staff, retail space and marketing and still make an adequate profit to remain in business.

P. Domjan et al., *Chain Reaction*, https://doi.org/10.1007/978-3-030-51784-7_5

In many developing economies, these basic currency functions cannot be taken for granted because of three key risks.[1]

Hyper-inflation: The currency is no longer an effective store of value because its worth is being eroded, nor is it an effective unit of account because prices are not stable. Price instability also limits the currency's utility as a means of exchange.

Capital controls: Regulations that limit the ability of individuals and businesses to exchange local currency for foreign currency or to take foreign currency out of the country limit the ability of the national currency to act as a means of exchange, especially for foreign payments.

Banking sector risk: Bank failures combined with the risk of loss and impracticality of holding physical cash severely limit a currency's effectiveness as a store of value.

Such risks have been a recent reality of life for people living in developing countries from Argentina to Venezuela, Nigeria, Zimbabwe and beyond. Historically, the main alternative to national currencies has been the US dollar, often operating as an unofficial market for physical cash. However, importing dollars only solves part of the problem, and can introduce new problems. For one thing, US monetary policy is designed to suit the needs of the US economy and may hinder a country struggling to make its exports competitive. In countries lacking foreign exchange reserves, dollars will still tend to be subject to capital controls, making the US currency hard to obtain legally and expensive illegally. For businesses, dollars still need to be stored physically or in banks, which might not be able to cater efficiently to foreign exchange.

Yet, despite its limitations, the dollar reigns supreme. It dominates financial and commodities markets globally as well as international trade—even when neither transacting party has any ties to the US.

Do the increasingly interconnected lives of global consumers warrant a global currency? Could bitcoin or ether be "good enough" against a domestic currency that becomes discredited and against a US dollar in short supply or damaging to the local economy?

While, for now, the idea that cryptocurrencies will become reputable global currencies remains murky given the early state in the development cycle of

---

[1] For a brief overview of currency crises in emerging markets, see *Currency Crises in Emerging Markets*. 2015. Council on Foreign Relations. https://www.cfr.org/backgrounder/currency-crises-emerging-markets.

these systems, it is not inconceivable that a path exists in the long run. To truly take hold in the developing world, cryptocurrencies need to outperform in at least some of the functions of money. To that end, we will now compare physical cash, cryptocurrency and electronic cash across a range of functions, ranking each for their relative strengths.

Transactions

The first hurdle is creating an accessible interface. The interface requires an internet connection, or at least a computer or smartphone for an on-chain transaction. By comparison, cash is the easiest form of currency for physical transactions. However, the efficiencies of cryptocurrencies far surpass often cumbersome electronic cash transfer systems.

Ranking for Transactions:

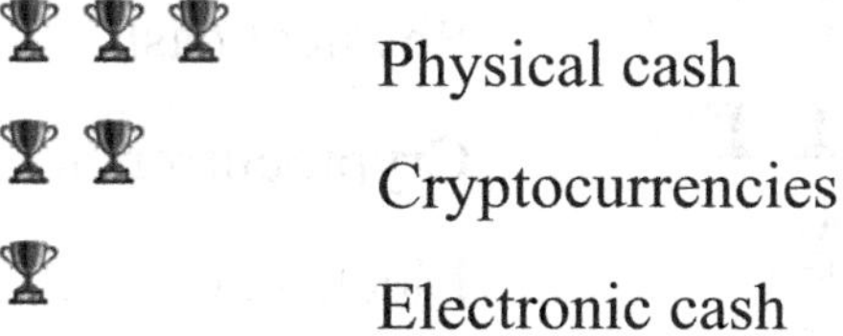

Settlement

Settlement involving cryptocurrencies is quick and final, relative to electronic cash transfer. If parties are in different geographies, the timeframe for settlement of electronic cash transactions can stretch into days and weeks, depending on capital controls, availability and other challenges. Settlement of cryptocurrency transactions is known and visible for all to see via the blockchain. Of course, settlement of physical cash transactions is immediate and final.

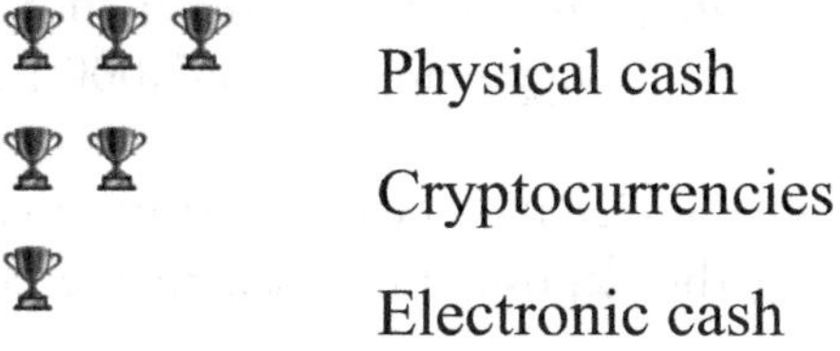

Handling

While handling of cash is cumbersome and prone to criminal behavior, especially when in larger quantities, handling of cryptocurrencies also has its risks. If you lose control of your wallet or private key, you've lost your cryptocurrency. The system around electronic cash enables handling to be as simple as having a piece of plastic on your person and a PIN. Yet, distance transactions rely on a labyrinth of bank-to-bank transfers and processes, opaque to all. The banking system, which is safe and secure in developed economies, is often less reliable in developing countries. Handling of cryptocurrencies is showing some signs of winning over even electronic cash systems, due to corruption and general distrust of local banking systems. As wallet infrastructure for cryptocurrencies matures and becomes easier to use, handling of cryptocurrencies has a path to being "good enough" in many developing economies.

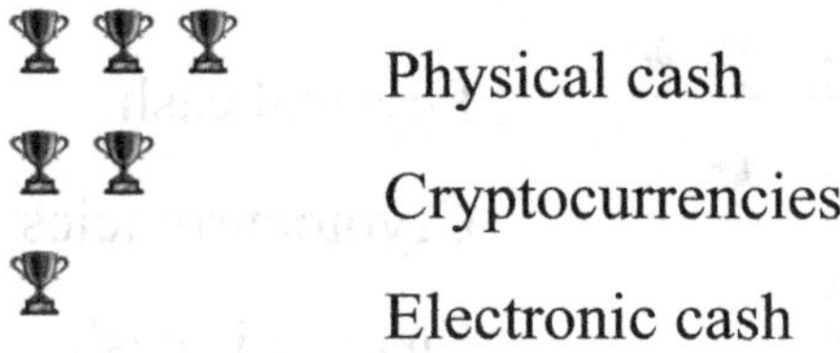

Storage

Storing cash is expensive. Even if you already have well-guarded vaults and armored trucks to move the cash, insurance alone is estimated to cost up to 1% of the amount stored in developed countries like Switzerland.[2] Such insurance is likely to be much more expensive in developing countries, if it is available at all, given the perceived higher risk and less mature market for insurance. Cash in developing countries also tends to be much bulkier because of the lack of high denomination notes. A standard briefcase can hold $2.4 million in €200 notes, just over $1 million in $100 bills, but only $250,000 in 100 Malaysian Ringgit notes or $47,000 in 10,000 Tanzanian Shilling notes.

While electronic cash is easier and cheaper to store, it can only be stored as a bank balance, leaving the depositor exposed to the credit quality of the

[2] Jones, Claire, and James Shotter. 2016. Banks Look for Cheap Way to Store Cash Piles as Rates Go Negative. *Financial Times*. https://www.ft.com/content/e979d096-5fe3-11e6-b38c-7b39cbb1138a.

bank. Although deposit guarantees guard retail depositors, they typically do not insure the much larger deposits of commercial depositors.[3]

Cryptocurrency clearly wins here. Storage of cryptocurrencies means preserving the existence and security of the public / private key pair—in the case of bitcoin, a 256-bit number represented by 64 hexadecimal characters. But this system also presents risk. Much of the hacking of cryptocurrencies written about in the media are in fact cases where private keys are nefariously acquired, allowing the thief to easily move the money to a wallet under their full control. Losing control of your private keys is not like losing your password; there is no recourse to regain access.

Some cryptocurrency storage services and large holders use a technique called "cold storage," whereby the wallet is generated and maintained offline to reduce risks. Only the public key is exposed online as the endpoint of the transaction. Like many aspects of cryptocurrencies, safe storage solutions are still in their infancy.

🏆🏆🏆 Cryptocurrencies

🏆🏆 Electronic cash

🏆 Physical cash

Altering or Correcting Transactions

For a cryptocurrency transaction, as for physical cash, reversing or altering the transaction once executed is technically impossible as immutability is a key feature and part of the design. The system that has developed around electronic cash has allowed for relatively easy changes or unwinding of a transaction, sometimes even long after the transaction has been settled. Ideas are being experimented with, such as escrow on the blockchain, insurance and other infrastructure to enable users to alter the impact of a transaction even after execution. In this sense, the current supremacy of the electronic cash system is more a function of the nascent state of cryptocurrency infrastructure than a long-run criticism.

[3] "Iceland Bank Failure: Which Councils are Affected?" 2008. *The Guardian*. https://www.theguardian.com/politics/2008/oct/10/localgovernment-iceland.

🏆🏆🏆 Electronic cash

🏆🏆 Cryptocurrencies

🏆 Physical cash

Acceptance

Acceptance of cryptocurrency is where the rubber hits the road. The two vectors with which to understand acceptance are between its global reach and the density of its acceptance within a particular region. The global reach of cryptocurrencies is inherent, given their internet-based nature. On this criteria, acceptance of physical cash is limited, especially once you move beyond the country that issued it. Electronic cash however is generally accepted globally: deep and sophisticated foreign exchange markets have developed to ensure transactions can be risk managed and appear seamless to the end user no matter what currency is employed.

With regard to how many outlets in a given area accept payment, cryptocurrencies are very limited. As compared to the ubiquity of whatever the local physical currency may be, cryptocurrency penetration has a long way to go, even in countries where the local currency is more challenged. Electronic cash, by contrast, has reached material penetration even in the most remote of regions.

🏆🏆🏆 Electronic cash

🏆🏆 Physical cash

🏆 Cryptocurrencies

Only after we see maturity among ancillary systems to support cryptocurrencies will we get a full understanding of whether they are in fact "good enough" to supplant traditional currencies in developing economies. Yet, even now, for all of their shortcomings, cryptocurrencies can provide some of the functions of money in developing countries while addressing some of the inadequacies of national currencies. Savers can hold their own cryptocurrency wallets without the need to apply to banking systems or manage the cost and complexity of holding cash. Cryptocurrencies may be less prone to depreciation and inflation given algorithms that restrict supply. In contrast to expansionary money supply in many of the most vulnerable economies, supply of cryptocurrencies is strictly limited. Cross-border trade in cryptocurrencies is harder for governments and central banks to restrict in the way they can with US dollars or other currencies–even though plenty, including Nigeria, have tried.

One of the main reasons that national governments impose limitations on access to foreign currency is to prevent massive depreciation, as all of the holders of local fiat currency tend to rush for the exits in a crisis, trying to buy the limited stock of foreign currency that the country holds, using a national currency that nobody wants. However, the same dynamic can happen with cryptocurrencies too: in order to have the benefits of cryptocurrency over local fiat, you need to first find someone willing to exchange your national notes for your cryptocurrency. In countries like Zimbabwe or Venezuela, where the value of local fiat has been collapsing, cryptocurrency can be as difficult and costly to obtain as US dollars.[4]

Case Study: Africa—Cross-Border Trade—AZA

What they did: Frustrated that a Kenyan, Ugandan or Tanzanian exporter can't transact with a Nigerian, Senegalese or South African importer without the cost and delay of routing payments via the US dollar, banker Elizabeth Rossiello started trading African currencies from her living room via bitcoin as a cheaper and faster common denominator.

How it's going: AZA now employs over 200 currency traders and other staff in offices in Lagos, Nairobi, London, Kampala, Dakar, Madrid, Accra and Johannesburg. More than USD 100 million of intra-African trades go through AZA every month, making it the biggest non-bank currency broker on the continent. Nowadays, very few of the trades involve bitcoin. Having created African currency pairs from scratch, AZA now has enough transaction volume to deal the currencies direct.

Verdict: The most fascinating thing about AZA's journey is blockchain's usefulness as a catalyst for creating infrastructure—in this case financial. While the ultimate outcome has been to evolve beyond blockchain, this would not have been possible without first building the market using bitcoin. The second most fascinating thing is that AZA is a profitable business—and there aren't too many of these amongst the blockchain startups set. That this should occur in Africa is significant.

---

[4] https://cointelegraph.com/news/is-bitcoin-really-selling-for-76-000-in-zimbabwe; https://bitcoinist.com/venezuela-sets-bitcoin-trading-record-new-hyperinflated-banknotes/.

While at an individual level cryptocurrencies may be attractive relative to the domestic currency as a store of value, any significant shift of deposits from banks to private cryptocurrency wallets will be severely disruptive for the economy as a whole. Reducing bank deposit growth could impede growth in the economy by limiting provision of credit by banks. In most economies, banks are the primary channel for intermediating credit into the real economy, transforming savings by households and corporates into capital to allow firms to grow (e.g. providing business loans), and enabling households to accelerate their consumption (e.g. mortgages and auto loans). Parallel systems for cryptocurrencies are still very nascent and not yet reliable options.

The flow of capital from fiat deposit to loan capital to interest and back again is not yet mimicked in any cryptocurrency system. Developing such systems for cryptocurrencies will take time. However, this is a short-term challenge given development is already underway around how to deploy credit systems within and among cryptocurrencies and broader blockchain-based frameworks. They may offer an attractive option for savers with a relatively high-risk appetite. The emergence of a central bank-sponsored digital currency could bring credibility from the backing of the central bank to a crypto asset and accelerate adoption.

Case Study: Seychelles—Financial Markets—MERJ Exchange

What they did: Recognizing that mainstream stock exchanges are too costly and complex for most as a means of fundraising or direct investment, co-founders Bobby Brantley and Ed Tuohy looked for a way to do things more efficiently to cater to smaller scale IPOs and investments.

How it works: Their solution was to use blockchain technology as a tool for recording ownership as digital or tokenized securities. In doing so, they were able to cut costs on various administrative processes to build a multi-product, multi-currency, cross-border exchange, reaching a wider investing audience.

How it's going: MERJ Exchange in 2019 became the first stock market globally to list tokenized equity. Beginning with its own stock to test the water, the exchange has since listed tokens for other companies. Next it plans to take on new asset classes—including a Ferrari TDF worth $1.1 million diced into a million tokens of a dollar each. MERJ's capitalization quadrupled in 2019—a rate of growth matched only by the Tadawul, which listed Saudi Aramco as the world's most valuable company—and was the fastest growing exchange globally in 2020. Not bad for a country of less than a million people.

Verdict: While exchanges in London and Zurich have talked about similar tokenized equity listings, it's notable that the tiny Seychelles was first—notable not least because of its location, off the east coast of Africa. Even accounting for lower GDP, investment by Africans in their local stock markets is paltry due to high broker and transaction fees. MERJ Exchange is showing how blockchain technology can streamline processes from issuance to shareholder voting, and create an access point suited to the "mobile first" ecosystems in emerging markets.

What About Facebook's Diem?

An interesting example of cryptocurrency's potential is Facebook's Diem, designed as a US dollar backed stablecoin for transactional use by Facebook users. Facebook argues that one of the main benefits of Diem will be to help address the financial needs of over 1 billion people in developing countries who don't have access to a bank account.[5] However, existing mobile money offerings, ranging from M-Pesa in Kenya to bKash in Bangladesh, are already helping to address this need. In most of these markets, anyone can buy a prepaid mobile phone sim card, and anyone with a sim card can load and spend using digital money tied to their mobile phone. An advantage Diem may have in the developing world is its link to the US dollar, provided Facebook can continue to prove that it holds enough US dollars to back the diems it has issued.

[5] https://www.bbc.com/news/business-48664253.

Practitioner Perspective: Financial Inclusion

Claudio Lisco is a director at ConsenSys, a provider of Ethereum blockchain solutions

1. **What's the big idea behind financial inclusion?**

For 1.7 billion people around the world, traditional banking services are not an option—whether because of distrust in banks, or lack of access to financial services in rural areas with low internet connectivity, or the fees being unaffordable, or an inability to present official documentation to open an account (government ID, etc.). This puts good financial practices such as saving, building wealth, protecting assets and participating in the digital economy out of reach.

Financial inclusion starts with efficient, responsible and sustainable access to a transaction account that allows people to store money, and send and receive payments. While this might seem trivial in developed countries, in emerging markets a large portion of the population is either excluded from basic financial services or has limited and ineffective access to them, with negative consequences on financial wellbeing and economic development. Access to safe, compliant and affordable financial services enables anyone to be a participant in both local and global economies.

In many cases, financial institutions and payment service providers have failed to deliver efficient and economical payment services in emerging markets. In developing countries, where cash is king, there is often less infrastructure for digital payments. In addition, domestic and international remittances account for a very significant share of the financial transactions in these regions, and so local and international intermediaries leverage their exclusive control of the legacy financial infrastructure to charge excessive fees for often slow, unreliable and insecure money transfer services.

In this scenario, blockchain protocols offer alternative payment rails that can enable a more "democratic," efficient and affordable access to transaction services, bypassing many of the existing intermediaries and offering transaction accounts directly to those who need them the most.

Many global fintech startups, financial institutions and NGOs have started projects to leverage the solutions offered by blockchain protocols to drive financial inclusion in emerging markets.

2. **What are some of the solutions for developing countries?**

One example is Sempo, an Ethereum-based Cash and Voucher Assistance (CVA) program built for digital cash transfers in some of the most remote regions. So far, Sempo has successfully been used to disburse tens of thousands of dollars at a time to hundreds of people—in minutes—at a near negligible cost. Deployed by Oxfam for thousands of beneficiaries, Sempo is used to transfer digital money via SMS, an Android application or an NFC (Near-Field Communication) card. The application is built with marginalized or disadvantaged communities in mind and has already piloted in Syria, Greece, Vanuatu, Kenya and Australia.

Another example is in the Philippines, a country where 10% of GDP comes from international remittances sent by overseas workers to family members. Unionbank created a decentralized, cost-efficient, real-time inter-rural bank payment platform that operated autonomously outside of existing payment infrastructures and intermediaries such as SWIFT and the Philippines' PhilPaSS. The platform connects rural banks as well as national commercial banks to the central bank, helping remote banks integrate with the domestic financial system while also improving banking access for local citizens.

3. **How does it all work?**

Individuals and businesses are given blockchain-based digital wallets that can be accessed via internet browsers, mobile phones—or smart cards for those in rural or low connectivity areas. These wallets allow individuals to conveniently store, receive and send digital currencies or tokens representing local and foreign currencies. The wallets can be used for direct B2B, B2C or C2C payments, and can also be set up to enable local points of sale using QR codes or Near-Field Communication connectivity.

Thanks to the global connectivity offered by blockchain protocols and their decentralized infrastructure, domestic and cross-border transactions can be executed in near real-time and at a fraction of the cost of the slow and expensive processes currently managed by legacy intermediaries. These existing payment systems can mostly be replaced with smart contracts that automate the payment distribution rules and enforce compliance and control checks.

In many cases local institutions and organizations (e.g. banks, NGOs, post offices, large retailers) also offer services that allow individuals to convert the digital tokens for cash, and vice versa, allowing the digital currencies to re-enter the economy as needed.

4. **What has been achieved so far in this area?**

Pilot projects such as Unblocked Cash by Oxfam have demonstrated the viability and the benefits of these solutions and provided a basis to replicate and expand.

At the same time, Central Bank Digital Currency (CBDC) projects are experimenting with retail distribution of CBDCs, establishing models that would allow direct cash disbursements to individual wallets. While developments in these areas are still in the early stages, there is increasing focus on such solutions as they could streamline direct aid distribution, something that proved to be extremely inefficient during the Covid-19 pandemic.

Unionbank's Project i2i is now live and facilitating remittances across remote islands and rural areas at a fraction of the cost and with significantly improved user experience.

5. **What is the biggest challenge to mainstream adoption?**

Education and knowledge sharing. There are still many misconceptions on blockchain and digital currencies that inhibit adoption. It is critical to ensure we are adding (not extracting) wealth to local economies by listening to local stakeholders' needs, empowering them to build solutions they can carry forward, and emphasizing accessibility and simplicity of user experience.

6

More than Money

While cryptocurrencies are a potentially useful alternative to national currencies or imported dollars, blockchain's relevance extends far beyond money. Opportunities fall into three main areas:

I. Providing services that require trust
II. Improving transparency
III. Data and institutions

Before we delve into each of these areas, a word of caution. Life in developing countries is filled with examples where moving from a manual, paper-based system to a digital process brings huge improvements in efficiency, but this does not mean that the new system needs to be blockchain-based. In fact, the majority of cases in question will almost certainly not need a blockchain.

From Paul: We hear enthusiasts dreaming up blockchain solutions for just about every possible realm of human activity. I was thinking about this while taking an intercity bus in Zambia. I bought my ticket in advance at the ticket office. Each ticket has an assigned seat number. As we boarded the bus, staff loaded passengers' luggage, ranging from backpacks and suitcases to sacks of potatoes and live chickens bound at the legs. Food sellers crowded around the bus, peddling samosas through the window. The conductor checks our tickets. If an assigned seat isn't available, he phones the local booking office to request a new seat number and updates the ticket. While the driver navigates the potholes and skirts around goats, cows and occasional elephants crossing the road, the conductor records which seat numbers are actually occupied and calls ahead to ticket offices along the route to tell them the seat numbers available so that they can ensure that they only sell available seats. The process is time consuming and leads to plenty of misunderstandings. With no centralized system for knowing who has bought which

P. Domjan et al., *Chain Reaction*, https://doi.org/10.1007/978-3-030-51784-7_6

ticket, finding someone else in your seat is commonplace. Children, live chickens and sacks of potatoes need to be shifted around to make space.

A digital process could certainly improve efficiency, even if tickets were still paper. Agents could consult a central database when issuing tickets rather than by phone. The system, whether analog or digital, already trusts the driver and the information she provides. Because no further authentication is required, there is no reason for a digital process to be blockchain-based.

I. Systems of Trust

Contrast the sale of bus seats with the Nigerian 419 scams we discussed in Chap. 2, where a fraudster finds an empty property and sells it to an unsuspecting punter, disappearing before the "new owner" has the rude awakening of meeting the original owners.

Property Registration

Could blockchain solve this problem? Or would a centralized database be "good enough"? Given the potential for an institution running such a database to be corrupted, this is a clear example of where a blockchain could provide a superior solution. Such a system could decentralize record keeping and create immutability of transactions and private-public key authentication of property records. It could enable a prospective purchaser to easily determine the registered owner of the property.

Even in developed countries, where land registries generally don't have the same challenges around corruption, such a system could be useful in reducing transaction risk and costs. In the UK, where ownership searches routinely cost thousands of pounds, Her Majesty's Land Registry has been exploring the use of blockchain in creating title tokens that could be used not only for record keeping but for fractionalizing ownership to make property accessible to younger and lower-income buyers.

Blockchain-based property ownership systems have been mooted from the former Soviet republic of Georgia to Bangladesh. None of these systems has yet made it to execution.

Soon after Juan Orlando Hernandez was sworn in as president of Honduras in 2014, his team began looking at restoring stability to the Instituto De La Propiedo (IP), the government agency that manages property rights in the country. The IP had been left to languish, allowing corruption and distrust to creep in. The government of Honduras in early 2015 engaged Epigraph, a startup applying land titling to blockchain.

Epigraph used the Factom blockchain, which focuses on providing proof of validation, or provenance, via a link to a transaction. The user would create a digital record of a document, video or other proof of transaction, and hash the record (as per the process described in Chap. 4). The resulting hash is then appended to the Bitcoin blockchain, creating immutable timestamped evidence of that version of the relevant document, providing proof that a transaction relating to a property title occurred in the past. At any time in the future, a person can verify the file to confirm or refute whether or not it has been modified. One altered pixel on the video or document would result in a different hash, not matching the original and demonstrating that alteration had occurred.

The same approach is being used by several large banks to confirm compliance with mortgage documentation regulations. The US Department of Homeland Security is experimenting with it to track whether videos have been tampered with.

Back in Honduras, within a few weeks of signing a letter of intent with Epigraph, the government itself became mired in allegations of corruption and the project stalled. Overhauling a country's property registration system is a long game; political instability challenges the multi-year commitment needed.[1]

Property registration has a problem in common with many applications: how to control the interface between the analog or offline and the digital world, sometimes referred to as the "bullshit in, bullshit out" problem. In other words, any blockchain system can only be as good as the data recorded on it. In the case of property registration, the challenge is in the details. For example, in the US, property rights vary dramatically in form from one parcel of land to another, let alone from county to county or state to state. Each parcel on the surface may have different access rights and other variants that can be difficult to understand, and even harder to digitize. Factor in details like height restrictions on a building or underground mineral rights and the concept of registering property becomes very complex very quickly.

Management systems for property rights vary widely. Australia, Canada and a handful of US states practice what is known as a Torrens system, whereby once a record is made within the property registration system it is considered final and in effect wipes out any prior claims. This negates the need for title insurance, as prior claims to the property are discounted once registration is

[1] Kagen, Matt, CEO of Epigraph, Author Interview, 1 October 2019.

approved. However, getting a record into this sort of system requires significant work to ensure the registration is legitimate. This can be expensive and cause a significant delay in transactions—sometimes months or even years.

Across most US states, an alternative system is used for titling, known as Abstract. Here, the county recorder accepts any registration as long as it adheres to the administrative rules. They make no claim as to the quality of the registration—that is left to courts and stakeholders in the registration. The county recorder is specialized to manage what has become an immutable record of all registrations, legitimate or not; the judgement as to whether or not a registration is in fact legitimate is abstracted to the legal system. This enables individual transactions to occur relatively quickly, as little is required aside from administrative procedure. However, title insurance is then required to cover the buyer against any dormant claims others may have to the land or any other challenges to the legitimacy of the registration.

When thinking about the promise of blockchain, the technology is only half (or less) of the equation. Understanding "how" data is enshrined on the blockchain is as, if not more, critically important. Imagine the chaos if 419 scammers could register their false ownership claims as records on a blockchain, thereby legitimizing the false claim.

For either titling system, Torrens or Abstract, the core of what is needed is a record of property ownership over time that is both authenticated and immutable.

All options to create a permanent record of land ownership are subject to risk of human error, corruption and maleficence. If the system is initially based on an existing land registry—whether digital or, as is more often the case, paper records—the blockchain will then inherit the imperfections of the existing registry. On the other hand, if the blockchain system attempts to start afresh, it will require human experts to inspect title documents, visit properties and make judgments as to the current ownership of those properties—a gargantuan task for any country.

One answer is not to focus on a state-driven property rights system, but rather to equip people with the tools to digitize their own informal system. Epigraph is taking this approach by open sourcing a simple version of their system that allows anyone to use their open blockchain infrastructure to manage ownership among a community of likeminded property owners. A system based on this would enable property owners to self-register and submit proofs of ownership, and then make these proofs of ownership available, enabling future buyers to make their own judgments about the property. The burden of loading data is minimized, and the judgement for validity abstracted.

Introducing blockchain means records of ownership cannot be easily doctored once they have been created. The system could be transparently inspected or verified, whether by potential buyers looking to establish the legitimacy of a potential property purchase, or by a bank assessing a property as collateral for a loan, or by tax authorities seeking to apply the appropriate rate. The provenance of the property could be clearly tracked—not just who owns it today, but from whom it was purchased and potentially at what price.

Clarity on property rights presents one of the biggest challenges, as well as opportunities, for developing countries. This is the key to radically changing the economic trajectory of a community. Formalizing property rights can have a transformative effect in unlocking capital and spurring growth.

Once property transactions are more trusted, owners are able to unlock the value of their property holdings, creating a major catalyst for economic activity that has been limited in significant parts of the developing world. Get this right, and the benefits to the overall economy are unending. Just think of the consumer boom in the US and Europe spurred by increased property ownership after the Second World War. The confidence of banks to securitize loans based on the certain knowledge that they could repossess if the borrower failed to pay is fundamental to the historic path to economic prosperity in the developed world.

The impact runs deeper still, according to the economist Hernando de Soto, who argues that capitalism can thrive, and overcome threats such as terrorism, only if legal systems change so that most people feel that the law is on their side. Creating this sense of inclusion requires many things, but one of the most effective mechanisms for change would be providing full legal protection to the de facto property rights that are typically observed only informally by poorer people.

Informal property rights cover assets—notably land and housing—worth many billions of dollars, according to de Soto's research. Informal systems of property rights usually render such assets "dead capital", meaning that it is hard to use as collateral for a loan to start a business, for example. Bringing these rights into the formal legal system will unleash this capital and spur growth. Such an efficient, inclusive legal system preceded rapid development in every rich country.[2]

[2] "The Economist versus the terrorist." 2003. *The Economist*, 20 January.

Case Study: Ghana—Property—Bitland

What they did: Tackling the issue of conflicting and duplicate property records in Africa, founder Narigamba Mwinsuubo has been working with paramount chiefs who own land in 24 communities around Ghana's second largest city, Kumasi, to provide 99-year leases to residents.

How it works: Bitland records every lease purchase approved by the Customary Land Secretariats that serve the chiefs of the 24 communities. Key details not included in the Secretariat records, such as the number of years of lease, are clarified on the Bitland blockchain. Where there are conflicts—say, an uncle dies and it's unclear which niece or nephew inherits—the family will meet with the chief to resolve the matter, with the decision recorded on the blockchain. A handful of disputes remained unresolved and therefore unlogged as yet. Once the information has been approved and entered by the secretariat, it becomes a permanent and accessible record.

How it's going: In total, 112 properties spread over 1400 acres are on Bitland's blockchain. But the project has stalled. Bitland is waiting on Ghana's federal government to permit a licence for it to operate. This is essential for Bitland to convince other chiefs and property owners across the country to provide access to their records and, ultimately, to use the platform for property transactions and security on mortgages. The not-for-profit has also run out of cash, requiring US$200,000 to keep the lights on.

Verdict: As in many other parts of Africa, there is clearly a need for clarity on land ownership in Ghana, where up to 78% of land is said to be unregistered. Yet the reality is that blockchains are reliant upon the consent and cooperation of the same politicians and their cronies who have for years obfuscated property records. And there's another issue too. Blockchains, which are meant to transcend any need for trust in humankind, instead too often demand a leap of faith to trust in the value of a token or coin. Bitland used a coin called "cadastral" to raise funds for its project. How essential was this extra layer of complexity compared with, at its heart, a relatively straightforward decentralized recordkeeping or distributed ledger exercise? "It was never a necessity," said Mwinsuubo. Bitland wanted to use the coins so people could issue land in tokens and create a record of transactions. Similar records can be created through purchases on established mobile money platforms, reflected Mwinsuubo. Projects already facing an uphill battle for official acceptance might do better keeping things simpler from the start, even if they fall short of the purist's definition of what constitutes a blockchain.

Does It Make Sense to Have a Blockchain-Based System Without a Token?

From Paul: Property registration is just one among many examples where value can be unlocked for society and individuals by creating a framework to facilitate collective action. In this case, the collective action is documenting and sharing information about ownership. Having a record of ownership creates value for the individual by increasing security of property tenure, reducing the risk of becoming a victim of fraud, and simplifying eventual sale of their property. However, this value cannot be encapsulated in a token.

Instead, the blockchain-based system is being used as a distributed database. So, why not use a traditional database? The UK has a very successful register of movable property called Immobilise, which is a traditional database maintained by a private company with the support of the police. This system requires the public to trust both the police and the company that operates the database to maintain the validity and security of the data and to ensure that it isn't misused,[3] and the police need the skill and time to design and implement such a system. By contrast, with a blockchain-based system, trust lies with the programmer who designed the system rather than with the local authority that operates it. One could imagine a credible international organization—or indeed the UK Police, with their experience of operating such a system—taking responsibility for the programming and deployment of the blockchain-based property registration system, allowing people around the world in developing countries to benefit through adopting a similar approach. Adding a token as compensation for using the system would just complicate a very straightforward use case.

From Brandon: If you want to take advantage of the full expanse of innovations unleashed by Bitcoin, you need a token. For me, the real beauty of the system is the incentivized effort. Each user type knows what they can and cannot do, how to do it, and is compensated for their effort. This allows for distributed work, decentralized ownership, and a very scalable system. Trust comes from strongly incentivized effort. If you are attempting to mimic any of these objectives, you need a token—not necessarily to compensate, but to represent the value as it is transferred throughout and generated by the system, and to incentivize the right, trusted behaviors.

II. Improve Transparency

Another set of opportunities made possible from exploiting the features of blockchain is around bringing transparency to opaque or misunderstood systems. Transparency is one of the much vaunted characteristics that

[3] An example from the developed world shows how important system design and security is in property registration: Strava, a popular app to share sports activity, allows cyclists to post pictures of their bicycles and share details of their rides. Given that many of the rides start from the cyclist's front door, high-end bicycle thieves realized that they could combine the pictures and the starting points of shared routes to create a database of high-end bicycles and their locations ready to be stolen. See: https://news.sky.com/story/cyclists-warned-to-beware-sharing-data-on-ride-tracking-apps-11273754.

proponents cite—building a shared ledger of who owns what, with transparency for anyone who wishes to examine it. Often the question to ask is what prevents current systems from simply exposing their databases for review. One of relatively few systems around the world to do this is the Swedish state, which provides open access to multiple areas of public interaction. For the most part, transparency for transparency's sake can be done using current technologies.

Like digitization, however, introducing transparency can be the catalyst to rethink the trust dynamics of a system, providing an opening for blockchain to play a valid role. Transparency may root out the corruption initially, but the corrupt always find new ways to subvert systems. Reconfiguring the dynamics around trust in the system provides a longer-term solution to address corruption and enable a more trusted and more efficient system. Blockchain is valuable when the objective is to reconfigure both transparency and trust.

Foreign Aid

When Afghan police officers started receiving their international donor-paid salaries digitally rather than in cash, they initially thought they had received a raise. What had really happened was that their superiors had lost the ability to skim off their salaries.[4] The problem of corruption and misappropriation is endemic across international aid. Greater transparency leads to improved outcomes.[5] Funds lost to corruption directly reduce the amount available to the ultimate beneficiaries of aid and also harm donor confidence, thereby limiting the amount of aid that is given in the first place.[6] The US Millennium Challenge Corporation and many other aid agencies limit the amount available to countries that score poorly on corruption indexes, and some refuse to provide aid to these countries at all.[7]

---

[4] https://www.technologyreview.com/s/427267/cashing-out-of-corruption/.

[5] Moon, S., and T. Williamson. 2010. Greater Aid Transparency: Crucial for Aid Effectiveness. *ODI Project Brief No. 35*. London: ODI. https://www.odi.org/sites/odi.org.uk/files/odi-assets/publications-opinion-files/5722.pdf and Ramkumar, V., and P. De Renzio. 2009. *Improving Budget Transparency and Accountability in Aid Dependent Countries: How Can Donors Help*. Washington, DC: International Budget Partnership.

[6] See Kenny, C. *Results Not Receipts: Counting the Right Things in Corruption* for an interesting discussion of the relative importance of corruption in aid.

[7] https://www.npr.org/sections/goatsandsoda/2017/08/04/539285319/is-corruption-really-a-big-problem-in-foreign-aid.

The World Bank is estimated to spend a third of its budget on validation activities, working to ensure that the financing and aid they provide goes to the intended recipients. Beyond this, 70% of its financing activities are "results-based," whereby the recipient is required to display the intended result as part of the financing terms.[8] The World Bank launched its Blockchain Lab in 2017,[9] with several pilots testing approaches to assist transparency and verification, mostly using the Ethereum blockchain. The projects have yet to convert to material impact.[10]

In guarding against corruption and demanding verified results, multiple donor organizations acting with the best will in the world often end up overloading low-capacity governments with the burden of overlapping funding applications and reporting requirements. Donors must also be mindful to coordinate in order to avoid targeting their funds on a relatively small number of key areas, leaving other worthy but lower profile areas needlessly underfunded, and weakening the intended impact.[11]

Donor coordination problems could be addressed by simply aggregating transactions across multiple donors. Overseeing entities or the donors themselves is possible by following the money. Identifying and tracking transactions is a means for both donor and recipient to not just trust, but also verify how money is used.

In this context, making the leap to build out a specialized blockchain to manage foreign aid is in many cases unnecessary. Foreign aid is a payment at its core, so existing cryptocurrencies serve the audit and traceability needs. Using Bitcoin or another existing cryptocurrency to provide aid would in and of itself generate an audit trail for interested parties to understand the journey money takes after it is given.

While greater clarity around aid decision making and donor coordination are undoubtedly beneficial, some actually fear the potential political impact of radically increased transparency. One senior British parliamentarian remarked to us when discussing using blockchain-based systems for foreign aid: "A blockchain-based system could work to ensure transparency in aid, but I worry that would make clear how much aid is stolen and that will damage support for foreign aid which, despite corruption, is really making a difference."[12]

---

[8] Hawkins, Robert, Senior Education & Technology Policy Specialist and Global Lead for Technology and Innovation in Education at The World Bank, Author Interview, 22 October 2019.

[9] http://www.fao.org/in-action/agronoticias/detail/en/c/903647/.

[10] Hawkins, Robert, Senior Education & Technology Policy Specialist and Global Lead for Technology and Innovation in Education at The World Bank, Author Interview, 22 October 2019.

[11] For a discussion of the problem of aid coordination, see Bourguignon, F., and J.P. Platteau. 2015. The Hard Challenge of Aid Coordination. *World Development*, 69, May.

[12] This paraphrases a discussion had under the Chatham House Rule.

Case Study: Vanuatu—Aid—Oxfam

What they did: In Vanuatu, locals are accustomed to burying their polymer banknotes for safe keeping. One of a string of islands at the centre of the Pacific cyclone belt, Vanuatu also suffers frequent volcanos and is on the earthquake-prone "ring of fire." In a pilot project to test rapid and effective deployment of disaster relief, Oxfam engaged money transfer provider Sempo and blockchain company ConsenSys to provide the equivalent of cash or vouchers to a community in the town of Pango.

How it works: The community received prepaid cash cards to spend in participating stores on food, medicine and essentials. Shopkeepers taking payment on smartphones via the Sempo app received tokens on the Ethereum blockchain representing cash for the goods sold. Sempo then totalled the stablecoins collected by each store and swapped for the equivalent value in cash.

How it's going: This is one project that expanded during the Covid-19 crisis, with the need for speed in channelling aid relief apparent the world over. The trial in Pango was on 112 recipients and 15 vendors, who successfully made 827 transactions, with transparency on use of funds but anonymity for the transacting parties through Ethereum address numbers replacing identities. Verification requirements ensured the targeted recipients received the funds and spent them as intended, with unauthorized transfers made impossible by pre-approving accepted users. Oxfam plans to expand the system to 5000 people in Vanuatu along with projects in Asia, Europe and Latin America.

Verdict: In recent years, the donor community has been moving away from giving goods and equipment that often are wasted and degrade recipients by removing choice. Instead, aid is increasingly provided as cash and voucher assistance (CVA)—but accurate distribution and monitoring is a huge administrative task. Oxfam's Project Unblocked Cash will help free up valued manpower during time-critical periods. Best of all, the blockchain technicalities are appropriately deep in the backroom, away from the user interface. "I thought it would be quite hard to use," says one aid recipient, "but as I went shopping, I could see that it was actually quite easy."

Case Study: Brazil, Burkina Faso, Ethiopia, Georgia—Aid—KfW

What they did: Confronting the amount of aid money and time that gets wasted on checks by donors and accounting by recipients, KfW developed TruBudget as a way of creating traceability on all activity related to each item of expenditure.

How it works: Funding is broken down into specific projects, for example, creating a primary school. These are then split into sub-projects, for example, construction, equipment, and design studies. Sub-projects are further divided into workflows, such as approval of tender documents, and disbursement of money. Each workflow has one assignee responsible for the work. This is the only person able to close a workflow. The assignee may upload proof of completion, for example, a bank statement showing disbursement of money or a report showing the curriculum. Once closed, the details are permanently assigned to the blockchain and visible to all stakeholders. As a blockchain entry cannot be deleted or altered anymore, each closed workflow (action) makes the author accountable to the stakeholders.

How it's going: KfW trialled TruBudget in Brazil and Burkina Faso and has since expanded it to Ethiopia and Georgia. The German government agency has made the system open source and free to access, encouraging other providers of aid or credit to use the system.

Verdict: The best thing is that KfW—disbursing billions of euros every year as the main development institution of Europe's largest economy—has enough influence for this system or others like it to become the standard for aid disbursement. Incredibly simple to use, this will save donors, creditors, charities and projects copious time wasted on form filling, filing and emails.

Health Records

Undoubtedly, health services need help the world over in the aftermath of the Covid-19 pandemic and, in some cases, blockchain technology may be a good solution. In many developing countries, health departments struggle to document vaccinations and medical histories. Health institutions in richer countries have been sharing trustable records and information for years. Many use electronic health record (EHR) systems. For these services, blockchains are a more recent development in a long line of tools to aid efficiency.

When it comes to medical records, blockchain is useful in three ways. Firstly, it provides a method to ensure secure audit trails of access to records so that patients and regulators alike can determine who has viewed records at any point in time. A second application is to control access: users of a patient's data often do not need to see everything about the individual. The system created by Amchart, a startup working to deploy blockchain-based infrastructure in India, limits access to relevant areas only for the patient and her medical team. The third use is to ensure the data inputted is trusted: When data is added or changed in a medical record, the identity of the person or system making the change is also recorded, allowing the individual to go back and confirm that the data is in fact true and trustable.[13]

Case Study: Taiwan—Covid-19—Bitmark

What they did: Bitmark developed Autonomy, an app that harnesses community Covid-19 information and data to help people minimize their risk and exposure to the virus. First trialled in Taipei, Autonomy provides users with a personalized roadmap on how to avoid exposure and how to maintain their health.

How it works: Autonomy builds on systems created by Bitmark to enable individuals to take ownership of their personal data. Applying this to health, Bitmark developed an app called "Donate" that empowers individuals to share their exercise habits, diets, sleep patterns, weight and other anonymized data recorded by Fitbit and other devices with medical researchers at the University of California, Berkeley. In another application, Bitmark built a system for Pfizer that matches anonymized patient health records to assess suitability for clinical trials. Autonomy combines environmental and health data from trusted institutions with private location information to help citizens and communities understand their risk and take action to reduce the pandemic's spread. The Bitmark Protocol secures information shared between individuals and institutions, keeping it private, while synthesizing survey responses with health kit data to assess a community's health.

How it's going: Bitmark launched Autonomy in partnership with UC Berkeley as part of its Safe Campus initiative to resume academic activities during the pandemic in late 2020.

[13] Quadri, Aman, CEO of Amchart, author interview 8 October 2019.

Verdict: During the Covid-19 outbreak, people were inundated with conflicting information. Many news sources are not easily verified, especially when distributed over social media. By compiling and synthesizing all available verified information about the pandemic within their communities, Autonomy empowers users to volunteer information in a grassroots way so communities can take action to protect and help themselves.

III. Data and Government Institutions

One of the biggest challenges for the world's most volatile and vulnerable nations is the destruction that occurs when governments change through coups, revolutions or war. Governments typically collapse in a centralized fashion—a dictator holed up in a palace or some other government building. As the leader is overthrown, the area is often destroyed, taking with it any hope of preserving records located in and around the area. The decentralized nature inherent in blockchain-based systems would ensure records prevail.

Alluring as this benefit sounds, however, it is unlikely to be realized in the cases that need it most. Dictators reign through division of power and control of information.[14] Durable, independent records, especially ones replicated in a number of locations, threaten the dictator's ability to rule the country through centralization and facilitate alternative centers of power. This hinders the development of blockchains, as official participation is required for the creation of any system that will ultimately challenge centralized power. Promising as blockchain-based systems might appear in supporting post-coup and war reconstruction, it seems unlikely that such systems would be adopted in the countries that would benefit most for the time being at least. Such systems would require concerted action by intergovernmental institutions or sovereign lenders to impose blockchains as a way of instilling good governance and transparency.

Identity

In developed and most middle-income countries, identity is taken for granted; enough institutions and physical systems are in place—generating national identity numbers, drivers' licenses, passports, national insurance numbers. In

[14] For an example of how Saddam Hussein used division to maintain his power base in Iraq, see Quinlivan, J. 1999. Coup-proofing: Its Practices and Consequences. *International Security* 24 (2, Fall).

poorer countries identity is a major challenge. India has created biometric national identities for its population, and Nigeria is working to do the same.[15] Privacy concerns aside, beyond a few exceptions, significant swathes of developing nation populations have to shoulder the burden of proving their own identity and creditworthiness.

The situation is most dire for those in the greatest need of help: refugees. Every time a refugee moves between camps they need to start over, as they typically leave behind any records of their identity, their medical records and their social connections. Here, digitization can help. Merely getting refugees' identity paperwork into a digital form makes transporting the records much easier and safer. Bandits and others who prey on those fleeing for refuge by stealing identity are less likely to succeed.

Identity is at the core of the opportunity to reconfigure trust in a developing economy. It is the basis of credit. Knowing who a borrower is and her past history of repayment allows a lender to assess her creditworthiness and extend a loan to improve her living situation or expand her business. Only once someone has verifiably established their identity, can they become financially included, begin to establish their creditworthiness and start on the path to economic advancement.

Financial Inclusion

Challah and Jimmy are brothers who run a guesthouse in Addis Ababa, the capital of Ethiopia. The country had the third fastest growing economy in the world in 2018,[16] and Addis is the most expensive place in Africa to rent a hotel room.[17] Across Addis, new high rises have been going up, their hulking shells surrounded with scaffold teaming with builders. Look closer and you see that the scaffold is made from branches of local eucalyptus trees tied and nailed together by hand.

In the midst of the boom, Jimmy and Challah's business has been thriving. Their guesthouse sits conveniently between the headquarters of the African Union and a stop on Addis's new, Chinese-built metro system, the first light railway in sub-Saharan Africa. However, even before the Covid pandemic

[15] https://allafrica.com/stories/201909260144.html.

[16] *World Economic Outlook*. 2019. IMF. April.

[17] STR survey, cited at https://www.iol.co.za/travel/africa/addis-ababa-has-the-most-expensive-hotel-rooms-in-africa-survey-reveals-30485954.

halted visitors, the brothers were credit constrained. Challah, who runs the guest house on a daily basis, has no other job or source of income that a lender could use to assess him as creditworthy. Jimmy, who lives in the US, saves and sends money home to invest in the business, but his creditworthiness in the US doesn't help to support the business in Addis.

If successful and internationally savvy business owners struggle to fulfil criteria for obtaining credit, the prospect for most is weaker still. Such difficulties are well recognized. Some lenders have moved to forms of social credit scoring, ranging from older models, where an entire village would guarantee a loan, to more complex models that assign a credit score based on mobile phone data showing history of payments, connections with creditworthy individuals, patterns of behaviour indicating regular work, and similar encrypted and anonymized information. While this works for microloans, it still requires a mechanism to establish and validate the identity and credentials of the borrower, and it is difficult to scale to larger loans of the sort that would enable Jimmy and Challah to expand their business.

A system that leverages blockchain, cryptography and other emerging technologies could address all of these issues, unlocking untapped economic growth. This could be achieved through a central register that would allow anyone to consolidate all of their financial data, making social credit scoring simpler and stronger. The system could potentially allow borrowers in the developed world to share their creditworthiness with family and friends in the developing world. Jimmy, living in America, has a FICO score, a type of US credit score. Assuming that his standing is good, he should be able to share his creditworthiness with Challah in Addis to allow Challah to borrow locally and expand the business. Whereas many blockchain-based models fail to work effectively because of uncertainty around the data uploaded to the system, in this case the original data would come from FICO, a recognized and trusted body, and then that trust could be extended from the developed world to the developing world using the blockchain-based system.

Case Study: Philippines—Financial Inclusion—Unionbank

What they did: In a nation reliant on international remittances for a tenth of GDP, yet where most people are unbanked, one of the country's largest lenders has been working with rural banks to service millions living in rural communities on less than $2 a day.

How it works: It's not just people. Many banks in the countryside have been almost entirely unconnected from electronic banking services and domestic money transfer networks. With approval from the Philippines central bank,

Unionbank's i2i platform has connected 130 rural lenders to access international bank transfers via an Ethereum blockchain managed by ConsenSys. Smart contracts enable users to pledge and receive digital tokens corresponding to Philippine pesos held in an off-chain bank account, and to transfer the tokens between themselves and redeem for pesos. A verified chronological digital ledger of remittances enables immediate visibility on cash inflows and outflows across each partner bank.

How it's going: Along with connecting previously un-networked banks, i2i has streamlined into a single transaction a process that previously required at least 20 steps to complete, vastly reducing time and costs. With an intuitive user interface, operable in low tech settings, the i2i project targets onboarding the remaining 346 rural banks, supported by the central bank mandating rural lenders to open up their infrastructures to enable integration.

Verdict: i2i stands for individual to individual, institution to institution and island to island. This archipelago of over 7000 islands presents a unique challenge for financial inclusion—and a massive opportunity. Receiving remittances more efficiently and safely is a first stage to accessing credit and other financial services. Next for i2i is to go beyond the Philippines to Singapore, one key source of remittances, by integrating with Project Ubin, another platform managed by ConsenSys for the Monetary Authority of Singapore to enable cross-border payments.

Voting

Preventing voter fraud, accurately counting votes and ensuring that elections are seen as free and fair are perpetual challenges for many developing and, indeed, developed countries: recall Florida's "pregnant chad" fiasco in the 2000 US Presidential election and the dozens of court cases over mail-in voting and voter registration after the 2020 contest. Legions of international observers turn out to witness elections in developing countries and to offer their impartial judgement as to what extent voting was free and fair. This problem has become so complex that commentators now sometimes refer to elections as being "free enough": not without voter intimidation or other means of abuse, but free enough to confer domestic and international legitimacy on the winner.

Trust in voting systems is a catalyst for stability. Distrust is a fuse for violence. Systems with more open, trusted architecture are under development through several projects. Such a system may make it easier to identify whether votes were added after the polls closed or detect similar nefarious activity. However, like many of the situations discussed, the devil is in the details.

The challenge with voting is ensuring the identity of the voter at the time of the vote. In the developed world, particularly in the US, the methods by which identity is attested at the ballot box is itself an undefined process. Some US states require photo identification, disenfranchising those that are unable or unwilling to secure a state-issued ID. Other states require only a signature of the (supposed) registered voter. The means of identifying those able to vote varies in some cases within states. Mostly, voters are required to register—complete a form to confirm interest in participating in the voting process. Others "auto-register" voters when an ID is secured, or other similar registration occurs. All of this is to say that, even in a mature voting system like the US, behind the decisions as to who can and cannot participate in the voting process is a labyrinth of policies and procedures, managed often at the local level. Digitizing even this aspect of the voting process is a Herculean effort. It would be naive to suggest developing countries would have a less chaotic or more defined process for identifying those able to vote.

Technology alone will not solve the problem of ballot box fraud. For an election to be considered fair, an appropriate mechanism must be established to ensure that each voter is able to vote only once and that everyone who votes is entitled to do so. This requires a whole set of processes happening outside of the blockchain, including monitoring polling venues and, depending on the systems of the country, either checking potential voters against a voter roll or marking each voter's finger with indelible ink to ensure that they do not vote twice. At the same time, any technical solution to address the problem of ensuring one person, one vote must also protect the privacy of the ballot by preventing any risk of information matching individual voters and the direction of their vote.

Solving the problem of holding free and fair elections requires much more than just preventing ballot box fraud. Even if the votes are counted fairly, the bulk of election fraud happens away from the ballot box. The party in power uses state resources, like control of media, to support their campaign. Opposition politicians and their supporters are intimidated or jailed. Candidates are disqualified, or obstacles are erected to prevent opposition supporters from registering or casting their ballot. And, even after the vote, elections can be rerun if the government does not get the result it seeks. While blockchain-based systems can help accurately count votes cast, they cannot ensure that the rest of the election is free or fair. Voting is a system; blockchain is merely a small tool that may be leveraged to improve that system.

Tax Revenue

Transparency in economic activity not only spurs more activity, but in so doing it may also provide more visibility for the tax office. This in particular can have an outsized impact on developing countries, which tend to be less effective in taxing economic activity. Large informal portions of developing economies result in lower levels of tax revenue as a percentage of total economic activity. One of the more extreme examples is India, where despite efforts to formalize the economy, tax revenue is around 10.9% of GDP, about half the levels in Europe.

The US, which chooses to maintain low taxes, is an exception for the developed world, as is Sub-Saharan Africa, where levels are inflated due to the combination of a higher share of mineral royalties subject to taxation and very low levels of formal economic activity in many countries (Fig. 6.1).

One factor contributing to low levels of taxation is the scale of undocumented and uncertain property rights.[18] Not only do clear property rights enable the state to more effectively tax owners, they also enable borrowing against assets and create incentives to invest in the property itself by ensuring that the owner will continue to benefit from the increase in value or productivity.

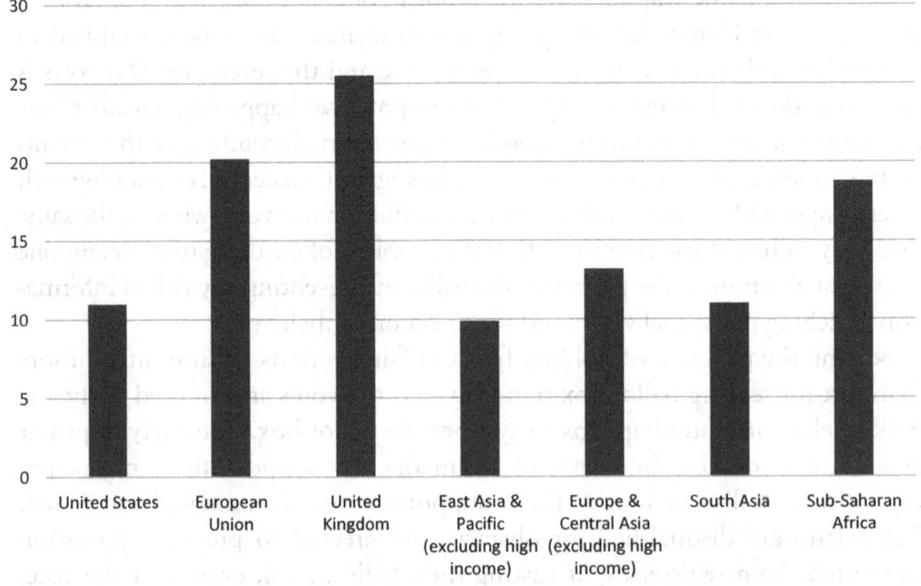

Fig. 6.1 Tax revenue as a percentage of GDP across various economies. Source: The World Bank World Development Indicators

[18] For a review of this literate, see Locke, Anna. 2013. Property Rights and Development Briefing: Property Rights and Economic Growth. London: ODI. Accessed 19 August 2019.

One key weapon in defeating the Shining Path terrorists in Peru in the 1990s was the introduction of formal property rights, which gave local farmers a greater stake in peace and the success of the economy.[19] While Hernando de Soto, the economist who spearheaded these reforms, did not use a blockchain-based system to deliver them, blockchains provide clear advantages for any government seeking to make similar reforms today.

Notarization

Notary services, essential to property transactions and businesses, are plagued by fraud in many developing countries. As with property registration, notary services can be easily digitized, with a blockchain-based system providing an immutable audit history. Notary services are in much greater demand in the developing world than in the developed. Registering a company in the UK can be done entirely online, as well as in some developing countries, like Rwanda, that have implemented extensive digital governance reforms. In India and many other developing countries, registering a company—like many other tasks involving public administration—requires multiple layers of notarized and stamped physical documents, and even where digital options are available physical submissions still persist in practice.[20]

Blockchain-based systems offer a better alternative to traditional, paper-based notary systems. Rather than relying on the distinctiveness of a notary's stamp to prove that the notarization is genuine, an entry in the blockchain means there can be no question as to which document a notarization refers. As with many of the systems discussed, the potential pitfalls lie at the intersection of the human and the blockchain: ensuring that data entered into the blockchain is correct and that only registered notaries are able to access the system.

By contrast, notaries are attestations of identity for an analog world. In the long run, blockchain-based documents can be signed with private keys known only to the holder of the identity, negating the need for a notary to attest to the person's identity.

[19] "The Economist Versus the Terrorist." 2003. The Economist, 20 January.

[20] "India Economy Profile." 2020. *Doing Business in 2020*. World Bank. https://www.doingbusiness.org/en/data/exploreeconomies/india#.

Practitioner Perspective: Tokenization

Jim Needham is Head of Strategy at MERJ Exchange, the world's first stock exchange to list tokenized equity

1. **What's the big idea behind tokenization?**

For us, as a stock exchange, tokenization means recording ownership or securing interests in assets on a distributed, immutable ledger. It automates transactions and other previously manual processes through smart contracts. It is about moving from paper ledgers, paper certificates and centralized and relational databases to a far more dynamic system. We see it as a redesign of the way ownership is recorded and the way value gets transferred. It creates the potential for one of the biggest leaps in efficiency since markets began. One of the gains that comes with this leap in efficiency is that it becomes viable for all sorts of assets to be securitized as tokens. This opens up a world of possibilities for new investment products and we have already seen a flurry of activity to fractionalize the ownership of previously elite assets such as artwork, real estate, collectibles, copyrights and so on.

2. **Why is it important in an emerging markets context?**

There is potential for a leapfrog effect in emerging and frontier markets in much the same way that we have already seen with telecoms and banking services with penetration of the smartphone becoming the single tool for banking and identity. Mobile integrates brilliantly with the technology behind digitized securities. For a long time accessing the capital markets has been dependent on having a stock broker or at least access to a desktop computer. Soon you will only need a smartphone. This opens the door to whole new demographic of participants. Emerging markets are the obvious starting place for this technology. It is harder to implement transformational tech in developed markets where you're competing with well-established, dominant infrastructure players.

3. **How does it all work?**

This is an evolution, not a revolution. Consider the old world: share certificates lived in the drawer in your desk. Toward the end of the last century, there was a move from paper records to electronic versions of certificates. However, the underlying approach was still the same and even though the ownership was recorded electronically, there was still a huge amount of record keeping required. All individual actors in the custody chain would keep their own records and these would be reconciled frequently—often with errors. Settlements teams at banks spend hours and days trying to resolve instructions that do not match. This system is ripe for an overhaul and distributed ledger technology is the obvious way to do it.

The system of distinct centralized databases, with all of their inherent vulnerabilities, would be replaced with a single shared ledger that records the ownership of securities as digital tokens. They carry with them a complete record of their characteristics and ownership history, as the token is passed back and forth on the ledger. The potential here is to remove lots of administrative effort, reduce errors, shorten settlement times potentially to zero and unlock significant sums of tied-up capital. It makes sense for the securities industry to move in this direction but there are significant structural reasons why it is not so easy.

4. **How did we get to this point?**

Distributed ledgers and cryptography are not new, but the way Satoshi combined them with new incentives and consensus created something entirely new in Bitcoin. If you think of Bitcoin as digital currency built on a distributed ledger, the next evolution was Ethereum which took the idea of a digital currency and extended the idea of smart contracts to broaden the application beyond just currency. Tokenization is really an extension of that philosophy.

5. **What has been achieved so far in this field?**

The biggest breakthrough really is that regulators understand that this is not a new asset class; it is a new technology. Like any new technology that might be introduced into financial markets infrastructure, there needs to be an evaluation of the benefits versus the risks, and how the risks are mitigated. Regulators are now having the right conversations.

6. **What still needs to be done?**

There needs to be much wider adoption of the technology. So far, things have been largely driven by application in the post-trade arena, which makes sense as the technology applies to clearing, settlement and registry functions. But the mainstream central counterparties have been slow to adopt it. This is partly because it threatens to disrupt their current business model.

7. **Given the enormity of the challenge, what is your approach at MERJ Exchange?**

We see the digitization of securities as an enabling technology that will underpin the next big wave of innovative business models, in the same way that Uber, Airbnb and Spotify were enabled by the use of powerful smartphones and fast mobile networks. As such we believe that more and more securities will be issued on blockchain and DLT networks, outside of the traditional centralized transfer agent and central securities depository (CSD) driven databases and systems. MERJ is connecting its end-to-end financial market infrastructure to as many of these networks as possible to enable securities and investors from all over the world to participate. This is why we describe our model as a truly global securities exchange. Digital securities will enable new business models that leverage the dynamic nature of a token. Whether this is in governance models, shareholder activation, rewards, who knows. It's not our job to design the models; it's our job to provide the infrastructure that allows them to succeed.

8. **What is the biggest challenge to mainstream acceptance?**

There is a chicken and egg problem. We need more quality on the sell side and more volume on the buyside. We are actively working on both sides of that puzzle right now.

9. **What is the biggest danger in terms of something going badly wrong in this space?**

The biggest danger is always bad actors, but securities laws around the world exist to minimize these risks. Everything we do sits within existing securities regulations, so this is the same risk that exists in traditional markets.

I think the biggest risk is probably a big powerful player adopting the tech in a way that, rather than being positive for innovation, freezes out new players. That would be a shame.

10. **Where do you see tokenization in five years' time?**

In five years' time I don't think we will talk about tokenized securities, they will just be securities. Within 10 years, I expect a wholesale replacement of the existing financial markets infrastructure.

7
Opening Up Trade

We've explored why cryptocurrencies may be a useful alternative to national currencies and imported dollars. We've looked at the potential for blockchain to improve trust, transparency and public institutions in realms from real estate to health and legal records, collecting taxes, elections, foreign aid and financial inclusion. Now, we look at applications to directly improve business practices in developing countries.

Counterfeiting

Street markets in Asia are famed for fake handbags and watches, but there's a far more sinister counterfeit trade problem for developing countries: medicine. Fake drugs are estimated to account for 15% of the global pharmaceutical supply, rising to as much as 50% in some developing countries.[1] This causes deaths from untreated illnesses and side-effects from harmful ingredients in fake pills. Loss of confidence in generic drugs hampers the ability of developing countries to create their own domestic pharmaceutical industries. Money lost to counterfeiters reduces the amount of available investment for drug development.

Nations rely on a combination of law enforcement, education and packaging with holograms, embossing and tamper-resistant seals. But it's not enough.

[1] Ramjiawan, Bram, Angela Ramjiawan, Paramjit Tappia, and Grant Pierce. 2012. Public Health Risks and Economic Impact of Counterfeit Medicines. NATO Science for Peace and Security Series C: Environmental Security 122: 203–212. https://doi.org/10.1007/978-94-007-2953-7_18.

P. Domjan et al., *Chain Reaction*, https://doi.org/10.1007/978-3-030-51784-7_7

It assumes that the customer knows what correct packaging should look like. In the case below, the shading of the box is wrong yet this counterfeit medicine was successfully distributed (Fig. 7.1).

The market for counterfeit drugs is particularly significant and deadly in Africa, which the World Health Organization estimated accounts for 42% of all fake or substandard drugs globally. Counterfeit malaria tablets alone result in 120,000 children dying every year across the continent, according to the Brazzaville Foundation.

It's not just consumers who can't tell the difference. Shortages in the system push hospitals to purchase medicine from street traders in blind hope that the medicine might be effective. Adham Yehia and Chibuzo Opara have both been running hospitals in Nigeria that they inherited from their fathers. Both tell of personal losses because they were unable to get basic drugs for their own families, let alone their hospitals' patients. They created a company called Drugstoc to help build a network of trusted suppliers and plan to build in blockchain technology to verify provenance.

Such a system will need to not only establish legitimate manufacture but also compliant storage and transportation. The WHO says failure to refrigerate Oxytocin, a critical drug to stop bleeding during childbirth, is one reason why a fifth of all maternal deaths during childbirth worldwide are in Nigeria, where medicine can cost 64 times the price in the developed world.[2]

Including a unique QR code on packaging linked to a register would enable purchasers to validate provenance. When the QR code is scanned, it would verify origin and manufacture as well as track its transportation, storage and sales. Any counterfeit or duplicate QR code scanned by a customer could trigger an alert to law enforcement agents tackling what has become a lucrative source of terrorist funding, according to the Brazzaville Foundation.

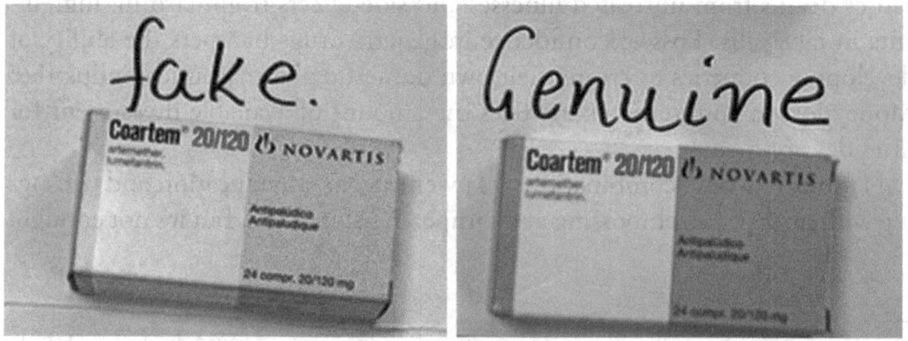

Fig. 7.1 Example of counterfeit medicine. © Interpol

[2] Information is based on WHO data and interviews with Adham Yehia and Chibuzo Opara by the authors and journalist Amy Fallon.

Case Study: Mongolia—Medical Supplies—Farmatrust

What they did: With a mission to end the market in fake drugs that is estimated to kill a million people a year globally, mostly in developing countries, Farmatrust set out to prove the provenance of licensed medicine by tracking and tracing every stage via the blockchain.

How it works: If at any point in the supply chain nefarious activity occurs, it is possible for a pharmacist to track precisely where and when it happened. Patients can scan the digital label with their smartphone and receive an instant reply on the authenticity and provenance of the drugs.

How it's going: The Ministry of Weights and Measures in Ulaanbaatar currently stands between Farmatrust and its pilot project in Mongolia as a test run for emerging markets. In a familiar story for state-reliant projects, it awaits government approval. Meantime, Farmatrust is expanding in related healthcare areas and is in need of another investment round.

Verdict: Farmatrust assures that records on its blockchain are "immutable and incorruptible." These words have an absolute nature. Just because something is on a blockchain doesn't make it immutable or incorruptible. It changes the dynamics, and perhaps makes it more difficult to impugn the ledger, but this is by no means absolute. With that said, there is an absolute need for a coordinated response from developing nations to rationalize the drugs market. It is a problem that will only deteriorate with the need for coronavirus vaccines and licensed testing kits.

From Brandon: While blockchains are not inherently immutable, some are more immutable than others given their structure and governance. Ethereum, the second largest cryptocurrency system by market cap after Bitcoin, with arguably one of the most vibrant developer communities, decided to alter their blockchain in 2016. A project from within the Ethereum community to set up a decentralized autonomous organization (DAO) was introduced, whereby governance over the system and community was to be integrated into the blockchain itself. In the process, however, a bug was introduced into the blockchain that allowed a hacker to siphon off US$50 million. Rather than allow the hack to persist (and due in large part to the fact that many of the investors in the DAO were also part of the governance structure of the system), the Ethereum community decided to fix the bug and "roll back" the blockchain to a state that existed prior to the hack—a state in which the transactions of the hacker did not exist and effectively restoring the siphoned monies to their original owners. In short, even the Ethereum blockchain is no longer considered to be truly immutable.

Overall, the biggest challenge for supply chain validation on the blockchain is that the system needs a trusted authority that can create the QR codes. In the case of drugs, this could be the original manufacturer, or it could be an industry association or a government ministry. Without a trusted authority to accurately validate the authentic products at source, the blockchain system risks reinforcing existing patterns of trade in illicit products.

Single country solutions, in which a government operates a registry and creates entries for locally manufactured and legally imported pharmaceuticals, are unlikely to be as effective as a holistic solution considering the large number of counterfeit drugs that are currently traded through illicit channels.

African governments have been coming together to tackle counterfeit drugs under the 2020 Lomé Initiative. Blockchain wasn't mentioned in the reported discussions. It should be.

Supply Chain Validation

More than $13 billion of gems are transacted every year through the Kimberley Process, established in 2003 to limit trade in conflict diamonds.[3] The process is a masterwork of coordination among governments, industry and civil society responding to loss of life from conflicts over diamond wealth, or so-called Blood Diamonds. Certifying diamond shipments originated in approved member countries with requisite legal controls and transparency. The Kimberley Process has become the best-known supply chain validation system in the developing world. As the Kimberley Process only applies to rough diamonds, several startups are working on blockchain-based systems for tracing the provenance of cut diamonds and other precious stones.

Supply chain validation is a variant of the counterfeit drugs use case, except that what matters is not whether the product is genuine, but where and how it was produced. Blood Diamonds have the exact same qualities as conflict-free diamonds. The same is true of other conflict minerals: illegally traded oil, beef from deforested areas or, indeed, eggs from caged hens.

The problem in common is that the supply chain is sufficiently complex that it is impossible for the end consumer to connect what they are purchasing with the original manufacturer and the links in between. Even if it were feasible to tag a cow with a QR code and record that code in a register, there are plenty of opportunities from the abattoir to the industrial and local butchery to the restaurant dishing up a steak, for the beef that was certified as

[3] https://www.kimberleyprocess.com/en/what-kp.

coming from a cow not grazing in a deforested area to be combined with, or substituted by, beef from a deforested area.

More lucrative than beef and even drugs and diamonds is the global trade in oil. Illegal drilling and siphoning has contributed to decades of conflicts and criminal profits across the developing world. Supply chain verification for oil has proven much harder than for diamonds. In the course of one voyage, a tanker may take on oil from several different producers, potentially in several different countries, and the ownership of the cargo is often traded while the ship is still at sea, sometimes multiple times. Legal cargoes can be topped up with illegal oil and customs officers are none the wiser when the blended cargo is landed. While a global system for tracking oil supply chains, or exports from countries that are at high risk of illegal trade, would pay huge dividends, the complexity of the problem makes this impossible.

Another market crying out for more sophisticated supply chain validation: vanilla. A byword for boring to many, at $150 per pod, Madagascan vanilla is anything but. The crop is more valuable per kilo than silver. Understandably, farmers go to great lengths to protect their harvest from theft, patrolling their fields with machetes. In a primitive form of counterfeit-resistant packaging, much like ranchers in the American west branded cattle to prevent thieves passing off stolen herds as their own, vanilla farmers mark their pods with a unique pattern of small pinpricks. Nonetheless, robberies still happen, with sometimes fatal consequences.[4]

Hashing vanilla pods to a blockchain-based system is achievable. Smart phones could be used to register the pods before they are sold to middlemen in Madagascar, dried and exported as beans. The equipment for uniquely marking each pod would need to be shipped to areas that can only be reached by canoe. But that's not the biggest hurdle. While conscientious local dealers and perhaps even importers and distributors overseas could use the system to check the provenance of the pods they are buying, there would be nothing to prevent unscrupulous dealers from still buying from thieves.

Across the Indian Ocean, Uganda is similarly blessed with fertile soil. In fact, the soil is so rich in nutrients that farmers have historically been able to forgo fertilizer. As agriculture continues to develop, however, Uganda now needs to implement a fertilizer distribution system, following in the footsteps of most developing countries. As African smallholder farmers typically lack the resources to purchase fertilizer, they are allocated an amount in return for a percentage of their boosted crop yields. But, as with any situation where the government provides something below market prices, there is scope for

[4] Kacungira, N. 2018. Fighting the Vanilla Thieves of Madagascar. London: BBC News. https://www.bbc.co.uk/news/resources/idt-sh/madagascar_vanillla.

corruption. Officials can fiddle records in order to sell subsidized fertilizer at the full market price and pocket the difference. At the other end, they can misstate the amount of crop that farmers have to provide after the growing season to pay for their fertilizer, either taking too much and keeping some for themselves, or allowing farmers to provide too little and taking a kickback. Either way, simple record keeping appears inadequate for the task of keeping this system honest.

From its starting point of no system for fertilizer subsidies, Uganda has an opportunity to leapfrog with a blockchain-based system to reduce the chances of fraud. Yet, as with other blockchain systems discussed, the weakness comes where humans validate transactions that happen in the real world and load them onto the digital register, perhaps understating the level of fertilizer that was delivered or the crop that was provided as payment.

Case Study: Zambia—Smallholder Farming—Topl

What they did: In a drive to enable the flow of credit to critically underserved, smallholder farmers, Topl's Catena, a blockchain venture builder, is using the Topl blockchain to record farmers' production histories across harvests along with evidence of good farming practices, such as their use of fertilizer, crop rotation and certifications on seeds—information which lenders can then use to assess credit risk.

How it works: Catena inspects and verifies farming practices and records the data on Topl's blockchain, which is then used to create digital, biometric IDs for farmers. Financial institutions can then use the information captured in the digital IDs to construct alternative credit scores for participating smallholder farmers, which can then be used to apply for a loan. Loan payments are stored on a farmer's hybrid payment-ID card, which can be used on merchant terminals provided by South Africa's PayCode. Payments can be taken offline and stored locally on both the terminal and the card to ensure redundancy until the merchant connects to the internet.

How it's going: At the time of publication, the project was set to launch with 3000 smallholder farmers in rural Zambia, with Catena funding the rollout. Concerns over food security in the aftermath of the Covid-19 pandemic have intensified interest in the project.

Verdict: Topl provides the infrastructure for a network where farmers can make, record and share provable claims with financing institutions, creating a promising inroad for financial inclusion among an otherwise unbanked population. The project can ultimately help farmers to move up the value chain and access new opportunities.

Case Study: Africa, Asia, Latin America—Invoicing—Trade Finance Market (TFM)

What they did: Identifying risk of fraud as the biggest impediment to credit for smaller companies and farmers in the developing world, Trade Finance Market, or TFM, developed Invoice Check and Collateral Check as a way for companies to pledge or tokenize receivables and collateral with creditors safe in the knowledge that the same invoice or collateral hasn't been pledged multiple times.

How it works: Paper invoices are subject to high value fraud—as a funder has no way of knowing whether an invoice or collateral has already been pledged for finance. Invoices can be presented to multiple funders and fintech platforms; the same invoice can then be funded many times over. This leads to higher defaults and credit costs. Invoice Check helps to de-risk invoice finance transactions by indicating if the invoice has previously been financed, using a chain of title and an audit trail of all transactions encrypted on the blockchain.

How it's going: A number of companies across Africa, Asia and Latin America have signed up to use Invoice Check, including Incomlend (Singapore), OmniBnk (Mexico, Colombia, Chile), AFEX Commodities Exchange (Nigeria), Crowdz (USA, UK), Iconiq, the World Blockchain Trade Consortium and the ASEAN Financial Innovation Network.

Verdict: Tokenizing an invoice results in a unique digital fingerprint. If someone wanted to commit fraud, they could change the inputs slightly, resulting in a different tokenized structure, acknowledges Raj Uttamchandani, Executive Director at Trade Finance Market. TFM has been developing solutions to detect when this occurs. Meantime, TFM is achieving scale. One Invoice Check client, Incomlend, for example, has partnered with CMA CGM, the third largest global shipping company, and another, AFEX Commodities Exchange, is using the technology to provide liquidity for smallholder farmers in Africa. TFM is also working with one of the world's biggest credit insurance providers.

[5] See, for example, Bernhardt, T. 2016. South-South Trade and South-North Trade: Which Contributes More to Development in Asia and South America? Insights from Estimating Income Elasticities of Import Demand. *CEPAL Review* 118 (118): 97–114, April 2016 and Athukorala, P. 2011. South-South Trade: An Asian Perspective. *Asian Development Bank Economics Working Paper Series*, No. 265. Manila: Asian Development Bank.

International Trade

Increasing "South-South trade" is the often-heralded golden opportunity for developing countries, boosting imports and exports with one another rather than with developed countries.[5] From the perspective of burgeoning youthful consumers, higher economic growth or proximate geography, this makes intuitive sense.

At the same time, barriers to trade tend to be higher in developing countries than in developed ones, impeding flows. The World Bank produces a score from 0 to 100 to assess the ease of trading across borders. While some developing countries, such as Moldova and Lesotho, score very highly, they are exceptions to the rule (Fig. 7.2).

On top of such hurdles, it is also tougher to lubricate South-South trade through the normal lines of trade credit, such as loans to pay upfront an amount of money invoiced so a company isn't left waiting weeks or months for payment, typically due from the customer only after a cargo has arrived and at the expiry of the agreed payment terms.

Blockchain-based systems can help in at least two ways. The most straightforward is speed and transparency of shipments. By the time a container completes its journey, it typically has 200 attached pieces of documentation. This can be much higher in developing countries. In East Asia, it takes an average of 58 hours to assemble all of this documentation to export a single container of goods. The same documentation takes just 2 1/2 hours on average in developed countries.[6]

The process is particularly challenging in developing countries because of the larger number of actors involved in overly bureaucratic administrations, the greater complexity of access rights and the heightened risk of fraud.

Digitized systems could significantly simplify trade documentation and make fraud more difficult by creating a timestamped historical record of each document and enabling differential access rights—for example permitting customs officials, but not competitors, to access certain documents relating to a container. It may also help with decisions on trade credit by allowing trade credit insurers to more easily access documentation.

[6]World Bank. 2019. *Doing Business 2019*. https://www.doingbusiness.org/en/data/exploretopics/trading-across-borders.

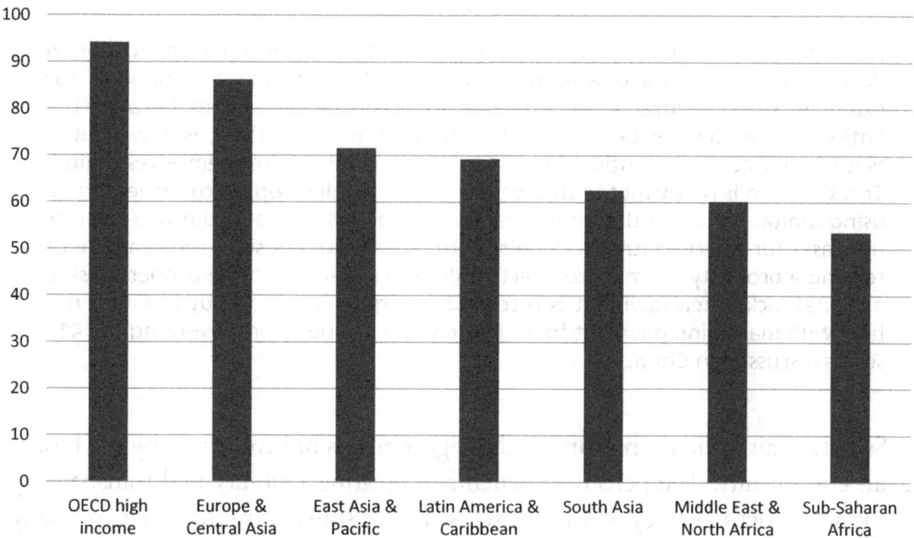

Fig. 7.2 Ease of trading across borders score. Source: The World Bank Doing Business project

The combination of digital currency, digital ports and smart contracts offers the opportunity to create a system of escrow that could make trade credit insurance redundant. The importer, who will pay for the goods with digital currency, blocks the requisite amount of digital currency against a smart contract. The goods are exported, and at each step in their journey, the location of the container, provided either by the scanners in a digital port or by a GPS unit in the container itself, tracks its location. Once the container is released from the port, the importer has a certain number of days to report any damage or problems with the goods. If the goods are recorded as undamaged, or the allotted time passes, the exporter is automatically paid in digital currency. A manual process of adjudication would still be required if there is a problem with the goods, but most cases could be handled by the smart contract without the need for trade credit insurance. This could enable South-South trade to grow even if trade credit availability remains limited.

The cost of building the system would be mitigated by reduced need for trade credit insurance. Companies pay at least $10 billion a year in premiums, according to estimates from Swiss Re and XL Catlin.[7]

[7] XL Catlin. *Global Credit Insurance Monitor 2017*.

From John: While smart contracts have plenty of use cases, their application in developing countries seems more limited. In advanced financial markets, for example, smart contracts are effective for financial derivatives because the entire transaction can be described using an algorithm. There is very limited need for human intervention. The actual assets involved are themselves digital. This situation is rarely met in the real economies of developing countries. Trade using digital money and digitally tracked containers is one of the few realistic use cases for smart contracts. Others seem farfetched. Consider the example of renting a property. A smart contract could provide access to the property using a digital lock when payment is recorded in digital currency, but it would not help with managing payment for damage to the property or preventing the 419 scams discussed in Chap. 2.

Supply chain validation is one of the bigger arenas of investment by the blockchain community. The perceived benefits of creating visibility and transparency about a product's journey from port to port have spurred multiple big company projects, from IBM's spinout TradeLens to ShipChain and Fr8 Network.

Yet all of these systems have limitations in truly opening up international commerce. Blockchains, particularly private systems created by big business, are not inherently transparent. While traditional databases can be made transparent with relative ease, transparency within a blockchain system depends on the technology enforcing rules in a clear and visible manner and building in game theoretic incentives that ensure good behavior, or make the cost for bad actors prohibitively expensive. Bitcoin is the only blockchain that has achieved such incentives at scale. In a private blockchain where such incentives are not part of the design, corruption may still occur. However, any corruption that does occur will be documented robustly, thereby creating a disincentive for potential bad actors. Corrupt or not, all participants are playing by the same rules, as they are enforced by code.

What all of this means is that projects attempting to bring transparency without also addressing the economics of the system they seek to supplant are unlikely to be "good enough." If transparency is truly the root goal, more tested, tried and true technologies are available to suitably address this need. Employing blockchain only adds complexity, technical challenge and risk to the endeavor. In our view, most supply chain blockchain tech falls into this camp, being little more than a glorified database.

The real opportunity, however, is to figure out if or how a permissionless system for supply chains might develop. What if no entity controlled who can choose to participate, be that as a supplier or transporter or other role? The system itself enforces the rules and ensures delivery as expected both in time and specifications. To optimize effectiveness, this must be the ultimate objective.

Practitioner Perspective: Data Integrity

Paul Snow is CEO of Factom, a blockchain solutions provider working on ways to protect and share personal data

1. **What's the big idea behind data integrity?**

Creating a set of data that multiple stakeholders are able to trust is challenging. Mechanisms have developed over time to build trust in such shared data. Technologies have provided for advancements in some aspects, but they also have introduced new and different risks. Often, in order to drive trust, a central authority is empowered to ensure data integrity, such as a government or corporation.

Blockchains provide a mechanism to document the expectations of multiple parties and provide a way of more fairly and safely creating a set of data from which it becomes possible to resolve a lot of problems that today are intractable. They provide a mechanism for a broader set of stakeholders to see and understand the evolution of data. Changes to the data are technically impossible unless such changes are logged on the blockchain. This visibility enables data integrity.

2. **Why is it important in an emerging markets context?**

The challenges around data integrity are not technological; they are political, social, cultural. Auditable logs, shared databases and other technology solutions have been available for years to support data integrity. And yet the trust falters among the stakeholders involved, in particular in lower trust environments, as sometimes exist in emerging markets.

Blockchain technology solves the problem of ensuring data integrity in a different way. Just as with other technologies, blockchain-based systems require rules and processes to enable data integrity. The difference is that, with these systems, many rules and processes can be systematized, or integrated as part of the technology itself, rather than managed outside of the software. As a public blockchain, the rules are visible to others, allowing for validation and ensuring consistency across the system. In low-trust economies of many developing markets, this alternative method of building trust may prove more effective. Transparency is the ultimate cleanser of corruption.

In such systems, institutions are no longer required to serve as the custodian of trust; the role is in effect distributed among system participants. For those that crave power, this can be a threat, as they no longer have control. For everyone else, this structure can be an opportunity, as politicians play less of a custodial role, and have more of an influencer or instigator role. The system serves as the custodian. Power is decentralized. Power becomes "of the people" rather than "for" the people.

3. **How does it all work?**

The core tenet of data integrity is knowing when, how and by whom data has been altered. Visibility into the chain of alteration of data instils trust. One such implementation is the Factom protocol. This infrastructure enables users to generate a fingerprint and timestamp for any digital file, whether it be a document, image or anything else, without any file size or file quantity limitations. This fingerprint is then hashed and added to a Factom blockchain. The protocol then anchors its chains in the Bitcoin public blockchain, piggybacking off Bitcoin's security and immutability. The result is an immutable, auditable imprint of the file's contents and existence at a specific point in time. Users of the system can use this fingerprint to create an irrefutable audit trail of their data for purposes of compliance, anti-fraud and other use cases.

4. **What has been achieved so far in this area?**

Blockchain solutions in general have proven very difficult to get buy-in from the "top." Participation requires acquiescence of some political power, forgoing some of the decision making.

Our experience in Honduras (see Chap. 6) serves to illustrate the challenges. The Factom protocol was to be used to digitize the Honduran property records, but the project stalled due to political turmoil. After that, we backed off dealing with governments and focused instead on loan origination. Coming out of the 2008 financial crisis, many mortgage lenders were fined billions of dollars for loan documentation failures. We focused on documenting the process in a cryptographically secure, immutable fashion. However, we quickly discovered that any mistake is then cryptographically provable as well. We tried to deal with the issue by providing methods to then amend the record. We were able to sell the idea that, in the long run, this provides for a cheaper, more efficient system. But the institutional fear of liability for mistakes proved to be a persistent barrier to adoption. The detail in documenting a process was viewed as carrying unknown risks.

Today, Factom is being used by the US Department of Homeland Security (DHS) to track the integrity of video surveillance data. The firm is also in the early stages of piloting a system to manage certificates and licenses for raw material imports that ensures the provenance of issued credentials, also for DHS.[8]

5. **What is the biggest challenge to mainstream adoption?**

The potential is there to apply blockchain to multiple aspects of our daily lives. Think of your driver's license. When entering a bar, you present your ID, which includes your name, address, even whether or not you need to wear glasses when driving. All of that data is shared in addition to the key data element, your birthdate. But even your birthdate has unrequired data, as the bouncer only needs to know if you are above a certain age, not your exact date of birth. In a blockchain-based system, the identity data provided ensures cryptographic proof of accuracy and can be audited by a third party if need be.

The biggest challenge is that these ideas require not just the technology, but the political and social will to do things differently. The power dynamic shifts. Incentives are different.

6. **What is the biggest danger in terms of something going badly wrong in this space?**

Much of the risk of these systems going off track lies with identity management. Bad implementation of digital identities is possible. Take the driver's licence example. Even in a blockchain-based system, the government manages the rules that govern who is authorized to drive a vehicle. The technology does not protect against the government choosing to share, say, your address with the bar you are going to, allowing that bar to then market to you. In fact, the technology might not just allow this; it may enforce this without your direct knowledge or consent.

Digitized data has brought with it a whole host of new problems around ownership and privacy that we are just beginning to work through and understand. Once upon a time, when people earned gold and silver coins, and spent gold and silver coins, the only records of transactions would be in ledgers, kept by businesses or people. This system of transactions and records provided by its very nature an expectation of privacy.

While we remain protected in the US and many other countries by a constitution guarding against search and seizure without a warrant, the records of transactions between parties are not just held by the parties, but the definitive records are held by banks, payment processors and increasingly by mobile app providers. In the US, the Bank Secrecy Act established that an expectation of privacy does not exist if the books are kept by third parties like banks and payment processors and not solely by the business or person themselves. While businesses and persons continue to have privacy in their contracts and agreements, once a transaction occurs through the banking and financial system, privacy ends.

Not only can the government access those transactions, they can require the banking and financial system to report those transactions as they occur to the government, even if no legally defensible suspicion of a crime exists. This is because what activates a "suspicious activity report" can simply be a dollar amount, divorced from any context. Governments are increasingly eliminating economic privacy in the name of protecting the people.

As blockchain technologies demonstrate, an expectation of privacy is possible in commerce. Governments are moving to outlaw such technologies solely because it limits the government's ability to ignore privacy rights. The goal is to manage economic activity in general, while justifying these actions in the name of protecting the people.

Blockchain-based systems don't solve these problems; they provide different means for addressing them.

7. **Where do you see data integrity in five years' time?**

The drive to deploy new systems for managing money and data coming out of the 2008 economic cycle faded by the time the solutions were available in recent years. Now, in the aftermath of the economic challenges triggered by the coronavirus pandemic, the solutions are available. The rails are in place to begin anew. I think you will see in the next three years an order of magnitude bump in the number of projects in production and affecting people's daily lives.

[8] https://www.dhs.gov/science-and-technology/svip.

8

The Big Bet Vs. Devil You Know

One common theme rings out from many of the blockchain technology use cases explored: while there are plenty of instances of problems faced by developing countries where blockchain might help (and others where it certainly won't), the most frequent sticking point is government. How will governments respond to electronic payment systems that could dent the national sovereignty of the currency, undermine control over monetary policy or, at the very least, prevent some ruling party cronies creaming kickbacks? How will political leaders take to disruption by a decentralized system that will make it harder to retain jobs for their patronage networks, let alone find money to reward loyalty?

Given the critical nature of the problems explored in this book, we believe that people will continue to seek innovative solutions and that blockchain-based systems will be the best answer to address several significant issues. Blockchain will be used when systems of trust are weak plus the conditions needed for a traditional or legacy system to take root are also weak or non-existent: in other words, when the value of the blockchain solution outweighs the value delivered by more traditional methods.

There are many examples in which we envisage blockchain-based systems being deployed even though conventional databases could technically solve the problem, particularly in developing countries.

P. Domjan et al., *Chain Reaction*, https://doi.org/10.1007/978-3-030-51784-7_8

Take property registration as one example to unpack what might lead to blockchain being applied in a situation where a database might be an otherwise perfectly adequate technical solution in a developed world context. The UK has a national, voluntary property registration database called Immobilise, as discussed in Chap. 6. The database is operated by the police, in such a way that anyone can register property by uploading pictures and proofs of ownership and recording key details, like serial numbers. Should you have the misfortune of having your bicycle, camera or computer stolen, the information in the database can be used to help the police recover the stolen goods and to expedite an insurance claim. This exact model could be transferred to a developing country, with a central database operated by the police.

However, building such a system on a blockchain, with open-source code—allowing anyone to review the coded rules and parameters—could help to develop trust in the system more quickly, especially where corruption and kickbacks are an issue. People might have less confidence listing their valuables on a database that could be seen by tax authorities or, in some countries, ruling party cronies, thugs and criminal gangs. The police might also, quite reasonably, have more immediate concerns than developing such a database.

The critical uncertainty which these scenarios seek to explore is not whether blockchain technology will be deployed in developing countries—it will—but rather who will do this, and what that will imply about how and whether the technology is used: Will the existing dominant institutions—banks, NGOs, corporations—embrace these new technologies to solve these problems, or will they seek to maintain the status quo?

We envisage two potential scenarios taking shape in the coming years. The first scenario, which we will call the Big Bet, is one in which governments and major companies in developing countries embrace blockchain technology to improve public services and serve their customers better. In this world, the police, for example, would establish a database, leveraging blockchain technology to strengthen and deepen governance.

In the second scenario, which we will call the Devil You Know, governments and major incumbent corporations remain sceptical of blockchain technology. This leaves NGOs and entrepreneurs using this technology to solve problems that governments have not been able to address.

Whereas the Big Bet is a world where blockchain technology helps to deepen governance, the Devil You Know is a world where blockchain technology is used to work around low-capacity governments and corporations that rest on their laurels rather than embrace new technologies.

The Big Bet

In the Big Bet scenario, governments and major corporations in developing economies do two remarkable things: they recognize that they have a set of problems linked to trust, and they look to embrace new technologies, particularly blockchain, to solve these problems. This is a world in which, with the blessing of government regulators, companies look to blockchain technologies to offer trusted services to their customers, and governments leapfrog existing approaches to e-government and go straight to blockchains to provide a secure, trusted service. The benefits are tremendous, but the Big Bet encapsulates a big leap of faith. Like most leaps of faith, the Big Bet does not happen as a single leap, but rather as a series of incremental regulatory and legal changes that collectively pave the way for blockchain technology to play a significant role in the economy.

Kenya's move to embrace mobile money is perhaps the closest example to something similar in the developing world, with demonstrable impact. In contrast to most countries, especially developing countries that heavily regulated their newly established mobile phone networks, Kenya allowed mobile phone networks substantial latitude to experiment with new models for providing both telecommunications and financial services. Mobile money systems are now common across the developing world, but Kenya is still recognized as an early leader.

Yet, embracing blockchain represents an even bigger leap of faith. Mobile money was introduced to solve one identifiable problem, namely how to exchange money in economies with limited access to banking services and often limited cash. Blockchain, however, is a new infrastructure for solving many different problems. In this sense, it's akin to embracing mobile technology as a solution for multiple issues simultaneously.

What does the world of the Big Bet look like on the ground? As blockchain-based technologies evolve, improved systems for identity, property registration and other use cases lower the barriers to participating in the formal economy. Combined with innovative approaches to credit scoring and continued advances in digital banking, the potential exists for financial services to more efficiently and effectively reach the unbanked. Meanwhile, blockchain-based systems accelerate the roll-out and security of e-government, making it easier for new firms to challenge incumbents, increasing the dynamism and productivity of the economy. Cryptocurrencies and widespread use of digital payment systems reduce transaction costs, remove opportunities for corruption and offer an alternative to the weaknesses of existing national currencies.

Trusted systems of authentication and record create a base layer environment that lowers barriers to entry and inspire new business models.

Blockchain technology in turn reinforces two other megatrends: the extension of existing mobile payments businesses into e-commerce channels, and reducing costs for companies seeking to embrace economically viable strategies focused on developing new products for the poor. Widening the formal economy enables governments in the Big Bet scenario to broaden the tax base at the same time as blockchain-based technology improves service delivery and voting, reducing political risk.

Consider the example of buying a motorbike, a common first major purchase for developing country households. Even if the purchaser has little formal credit history, in the Big Bet scenario their use of digital money and their blockchain-based single national identity form the basis for a bank to make an informed lending decision. Having secured a loan, the purchaser continues to build a credit history. Because the purchase has been formalized and is linked to the buyer's digital identity, it is straightforward for the government to charge VAT on the purchase, expanding the tax base. The introduction of these digital channels also reduces barriers to the bank serving customers like our borrower, expanding the bank's revenue and margins. This leads to the bank making both more loans, thereby supporting economic growth, and more profit, thereby increasing the tax paid by the bank. The title of the motorcycle is held electronically on a blockchain-based property register. Eventually, when the owner is ready to sell the motorcycle and buy a car, the buyer of the used motorbike can use that property registration to verify the ownership of the motorcycle and whether the original loan guaranteed by the bike remains outstanding.

Moving from cash to digital payments with cryptocurrency also helps to reduce the risk of theft and support transactions. From Central Asia to Central Africa, major purchases are frequently made with huge stacks of low denomination bank notes. The process often involves having to travel many hours to a bank to obtain the notes in the first place. In Malawi, for example, the largest denomination note is worth US$2.75, so even the purchase of a used motorcycle might require a stack of more than 150 notes. In some of Malawi's more economically successful communities, such as fishing villages on the islands in Lake Malawi, a prospective purchaser would need to travel five hours each way on a weekly, frequently delayed colonial-era ferry to withdraw the money to purchase the motorbike. The complexity of getting cash complicates and sometimes prevents transactions from taking place. Cryptocurrencies and other digital money solutions are clearly an appealing alternative, and official support for cryptocurrencies would help to encourage mobile operators and banks to facilitate bringing this technology to a wider population.[1]

The Devil You Know

Just as the Big Bet scenario is the sum of many small choices, the Devil You Know scenario also unfolds in a sequential manner. Rather than embracing something new, governments and incumbent corporations stick to existing systems, technologies and approaches: "better the devil you know." Governments gradually introduce wide-ranging regulation that clamps down on the use of cryptocurrencies and blockchain technology in order both to "protect" the public from cryptocurrency volatility and to respond to various high-profile cases of cryptocurrencies being used to evade taxes, circumvent foreign exchange controls, launder money and otherwise subvert the state's role in managing effective monetary policy. This regulatory clampdown in pariah states, like Venezuela and Zimbabwe, serves only to remove a potential pathway out of economic collapse. The need is also particularly felt in countries like Nigeria and Kenya, where bitcoin represents a relatively large share of GDP.[2]

Even if blockchain technology is not explicitly targeted by regulation, the presumption of official resistance leads domestic businesses and financial institutions in developing countries to choose not to invest in blockchain-based solutions. Instead, they emulate the model of centralized trust used in developed countries. With the risk of competition from new blockchain-based business models apparently removed, incumbents are under less pressure to innovate and improve.

Meanwhile the public in developing economies continues to use blockchain technology to solve the real problems of their daily lives, adopting technology solutions from overseas to adapt to the lack of trust in their own societies. For example, it might become increasingly common in Bangladesh and Nigeria, which rank among the most difficult countries in the world in which to register property, for people to register their property using digital

[1] While smartphone penetration is growing rapidly in sub-Saharan Africa, it still stood at only 33% in 2018, with much lower levels in some countries (http://www.itwebafrica.com/mobilex/320-south-africa/244990-sub-saharan-africas-smartphone-penetration-at-33). Levels in South Asia can be even lower, at 34% in Pakistan (https://www.statista.com/statistics/671542/smartphone-penetration-as-share-of-connections-in-pakistan/) and 24% in India (https://venturebeat.com/2019/02/05/pew-south-korea-has-the-worlds-highest-smartphone-ownership-rate/).

[2] World Bank data, LocalBitcoins.com and author analysis.

asset platforms based in the West rather than, or at least in addition to, the official centralized systems in their own countries.

As blockchain technology continues to develop, it becomes increasingly difficult for governments to maintain economic restrictions and control. Without the ability to rely on official institutions of trust, much of developing nations' economic activity remains in the informal economy and the availability of non-state systems of trust allow that economic activity to deepen in sophistication. This undermines both the government's ability to tax and, as more assets are held in possibly elicit cryptocurrency form rather than in banks, the financial system's ability to intermediate credit to the real economy.

Consider the same motorcycle purchase in the world of the Devil You Know. While the purchaser has a meaningful financial history in their various cryptocurrency and mobile money transactions, the lack of official support for these digital channels means that this history cannot be used by a locally regulated bank as the basis for a loan. Instead, the purchaser is forced to take several unsecured loans from fintechs that are equipped to use this financial history to make a credit decision. Without a national digital identity, it is difficult for anyone other than the borrower herself to assess her total indebtedness, raising the risk of excessive borrowing. Lenders compensate for this risk with higher interest rates. Loans are disbursed in both cryptocurrency and mobile money that can be withdrawn as cash from local agents, pending availability of actual notes.

Once the purchaser has assembled the balance to purchase the motorcycle, she does so using a combination of cryptocurrency, physical cash and mobile money. She checks ownership of the motorcycle using a blockchain-based digital asset registration platform based in Europe that offers free service for registration of low-value (by Western standards) assets to consumers in the developing world. Having completed the purchase, the new owner registers the motorcycle in her own name on the same overseas platform. Because the actual motorcycle purchase happens informally, no tax is paid. Rather the government imposes transaction taxes on those fintechs and mobile money providers that come under its purview.

As in the world of the Big Bet, blockchain technology enables a motorcycle purchase that might not otherwise have happened, increasing the welfare and improving the economic prospects of the new owner. However, whereas in the Big Bet, blockchain technology enables this purchase through official channels, in the Devil You Know scenario, blockchain technology pushes the borrower to work around official channels to purchase and register the motorcycle.

Where Will These Scenarios Unfold?

In both the Big Bet and the Devil You Know scenarios, the advantages of blockchain technology mean that the share of the blockchain-enabled economy continues to grow. The main difference is this: In the Big Bet, governments and companies embrace the blockchain-enabled economy, and as the new economy built on blockchain technology grows, so does the share of the formal economy, creating a virtuous cycle. By contrast, in the Devil You Know scenario, blockchain technology exists predominantly in the informal economy, creating a vicious cycle in which existing weak institutions are undermined as people choose new blockchain-based informal alternatives.

Which of these scenarios will eventuate? Undoubtedly both of them will, but in different places as each country responds in its own way to this new and potentially powerfully transformative technology. Ambitious governments will embrace the Big Bet, but too many will hew closely to the Devil You Know, depriving their citizens, and themselves, of the wider political and economic benefits that blockchain technology could deliver. Sadly, we are beginning to see the signs already of some countries—notably Nigeria—adopting the Devil You Know approach. There is a critical role here for intergovernmental institutions, NGOs, and global leaders and influencers to champion the permanent transition made possible by technology to a world in which transparency keeps business honest and holds government to account.

Conclusion

The coronavirus pandemic has brought into focus many of the problems that blockchain technology could help solve in novel, more effective ways—but also the fundamental tensions about how governments and society embrace new technologies (or not). Covid-19 has accelerated digitization across the board, and blockchain technology provides opportunity to optimize this shift. The key question remains how this technology will be deployed and by whom.

Consider contact tracing. The world has yet to agree who should be responsible for contract tracing and how it should work. In developed countries, various Ministries of Health have pursued workable contact tracing systems, whether through development in-house or relying on the Apple/Google contact tracing notification system. Most developing countries lack the capacity to develop such a system on their own and, if they were able, the public may not trust it enough to use it.

By offering a verifiable security and trust architecture, blockchain-based systems could bridge this gap in several ways. Individual governments could use blockchain-based systems to build trust in their homegrown solutions by including NGOs and other trusted parties in development and execution. Such systems can help to beat Covid-19 and build an infrastructure to respond to future epidemics, while also providing novel structures designed to protect users' data.

P. Domjan et al., *Chain Reaction*, https://doi.org/10.1007/978-3-030-51784-7

Managing property ownership is another area upended by Covid-19. When governments from London to Pennsylvania implementing the first Covid-19 lockdowns decided that property transactions are not "essential services," the entire industry ground to a halt. For several months, all property transactions ceased. In parallel, a great migration was beginning, as city dwellers realized that they no longer had to stay in town and could move to the countryside for a different pace and way of life. Demand for property was in effect put in a box, held up by the shutdown.

As property transactions restarted, the floodgates opened. Land that had sat on the market for years was now getting multiple offers. Homes were sold sight unseen, also with multiple offers. Agents, title companies and the rest of the real estate apparatus went from business as usual, to complete shutdown, to an absolute frenetic pace.

This experience highlights the weaknesses of a system where people are forced to physically participate in what is in reality a non-physical verification process—the transfer of property ownership from the current bone fide incumbent owner to the next. The lack of a digital infrastructure is a weakness of the system that was exposed by the Covid-19 lockdowns. Blockchain is not the panacea, but it can be the catalyst to effectively and efficiently move processes and procedures that today are still rooted in the physical, analog world into the digital age.

Money is another case in point. While many around the world have already made the transition to electronic money, whether credit cards, mobile money or cryptocurrencies, a huge number of people globally, and especially in the developing world, remain without access to electronic means of payment. The unbanked are between a rock and a hard place. Without bank accounts, they cannot access electronic payments upon which much of the modern world depends. This leaves them cut off from a wide range of digital services and e-commerce, at constant risk of theft and, with Covid-19, exposed to cash as a vector of infection.

As Covid-19 struck, countries rushed to give the unbanked access to electronic payments. Across the emerging markets, regulators capped fees on mobile money and required more businesses to use it. Kenya even tried to force *matatus*, the ubiquitous shared van taxis that ply their trade on the streets of Africa, which have long depended on cash to avoid reporting their income to the tax authorities, to shift all payments to mobile money. The *matatus* embraced hand sanitizer and face masks, but paying tax was a bridge too far.

In the UK, the government turned to lightly regulated fintechs to provide card payments to society's most vulnerable. The Salvation Army and other charities, which distribute UK government support payments to victims of human trafficking and modern slavery, switched from handing out cash to prepaid cards. Sadly, many of those cards were ultimately operated by Wirecard, a fraudulent German payments behemoth that collapsed in the summer of 2020. Beneficiaries went hungry during the four days that Wirecard's UK operations were frozen, unable to buy food without their £35 weekly support payment. Digital infrastructure, particularly when dependent on third-party intermediaries, has weaknesses, too.

Covid-19 has provided fresh impetus to remove physical currency from society, but even in the UK and Kenya we see that removing cash from the equation entirely is unlikely. If the world is going to eliminate physical currency, it will need digital currencies to replace it. And those digital currencies, whether today's cryptocurrencies or Central Bank-backed digital currencies, will almost certainly be built on blockchain technology.

In the first chapter of this book, we used Clayton Christensen's framework for innovation to explain why blockchain technology would have its greatest impact in the developing world: New innovations are accepted when they are good enough to replace the existing technology, and that bar of "good enough" is much lower in developing countries, which often have weaker institutions and pressing problems. Covid-19 will accelerate this creative destruction. Weak public health information tools and filthy circulating cash were good enough before Covid-19, but they aren't anymore. Falling revenue and remote working mean that, for many companies, manual processes that might have been clunky but good enough in the past are no longer acceptable; they will have to become digital. When most of the business is already digital, as is often the case in developed countries, the incentive to experiment with a new architecture, like a blockchain-based system, is low. But when an emerging market company or government ministry decides to digitize its processes for the first time, it can move directly to the most suitable technology available today. For the many reasons that we argue in this book, that most suitable technology will often be based on blockchain technology.

The post-Covid world may be filled with shadow as we slowly recover from the pandemic, but the blockchain future remains brighter, and as complicated, as it ever was. We're now hurtling towards a blockchain-based future even faster.

Index[1]

A
Abstract system, 60
Addis Ababa, 70
Africa, 2, 51, 53, 62, 70, 80, 85, 102
Amchart, 68
Apple, 3, 101
Application-specific integrated circuits (ASICs), 32, 33
Argentina, 25, 46
ARPANET, 18
Asean Financial Innovation Network, 85
Asset-backed Token, 37
Australia, 59
Authentication, 58, 96
Auto loans, 52
AZA, 51
Azure Blockchain Service, 35

B
Bangladesh, 53, 58, 97
Bextmachine, 35
Bitcoin
  Bitcoin: A Peer-to-Peer Electronic Cash System, 7
  community, 18, 26, 29, 34, 38
  Core, 28, 29, 29n3
  node, 27
Bitcoiners, 18
Bitland, 62
Bitmark
  autonomy app, 68
  donate, 68
  protocol, 68
Bkash, 53
Blockchain
  blockchain-based systems, 5, 14, 63, 65, 69, 71, 73, 75, 82–84, 86, 93, 95, 101, 103
  community, 7, 18, 60, 88
  technology, 7, 15, 16, 18, 34–36, 52, 53, 60, 80, 88, 93–99, 101, 103
Block creation, 30
Block reward, 29, 31, 32
Blood diamonds, 82
Brantley, Bobby, 52
Brazil, 67
Brazzaville Foundation, 80
Burkina Faso, 67

[1] Note: Page numbers followed by 'n' refer to notes.

P. Domjan et al., *Chain Reaction*, https://doi.org/10.1007/978-3-030-51784-7

C
Cadastral, 62
Canada, 59
Capital controls, 46, 47
Cash and voucher assistance (CVA), 66
Catena, 84
Cede & Co., 16
Central Asia, 96
China, 3, 12
Coda Coffee Co., 35
Collateral Check, 85
Commodities, 25, 37, 46
Consensus, 17, 31, 39
Consensys, 20, 66
Costa Rica, 35
Counterfeiting, 79–84
Covid-19, 17, 66, 68, 84, 101–103
Credit score, 71, 84
Crypto community, 7
Cryptocurrencies, 7, 15, 25, 27, 34, 37, 38, 45, 47–52, 57, 65, 79, 95–98, 102, 103
Cryptography, 7, 31, 71
Cryptokitties, 36, 38
Currencies, 8, 10, 25, 26, 33, 37, 45–47, 46n1, 50–52, 57, 79, 87, 93, 95, 103

D
de Soto, Hernando, 61, 75
Dead capital, 61
Decentralized, 7, 28, 38, 69, 93
Decentralized autonomous organization (DAO), 38
Depository Trust and Clearing Corporation (DTCC), 16
Depreciation, 50, 51
Developing markets, 38
Difficulty adjustment, 30
Directed acyclic graph (DAG), 39
Distributed database, 63
Distributed Ledger Technology (DLT), 7
Dobson, Samuel, 28
Dole Foods, 16
Drugstoc, 80

E
East Asia, 86
Elections, 10, 72, 73, 79
Electronic cash, 47–50
Electronic cash transfer systems, 47
Emerging markets, 8, 46n1, 53, 81, 103
Energy, 26, 31, 31n4
Epigraph, 59, 60
Ether, 27
Ethereum, 20, 26, 27, 31, 36–38, 46, 65, 66, 72
  community, 38
Ethiopia, 67, 70
Europe, 61, 66, 67, 74, 98

F
Facebook, 38, 53
Factom
  blockchain, 59
  protocol, 88–91
Falke, Marco, 28
Farmatrust, 81
Ferrari, 53
Fiat, 25, 33, 34, 36–38, 51, 52
Fiat currencies, 25, 26, 33, 34, 51
FICO score, 71
Financial inclusion, 4, 70–72, 79, 84
Fintechs, 85, 98, 102
Fitbit, 68
Foreign aid, 64–67, 79
419, 11, 38, 58, 60
  Beware 419, 11
Fr8 Network, 88
Frontier, 5, 7, 10
Frontier markets, 5, 7

G
Georgia, 5, 58, 67
Ghana, 62
Global Financial Crisis, 15
Gold, 6, 25, 34, 37
Good enough, 1–8, 16, 36, 48, 50, 58, 88, 103
Google, 19, 101
Government sponsored e-money, 38
Greece, 12, 13
Gross Domenstic Product (GDP), 53, 71, 74, 97

H
Hala Systems, 20
Hash function, 29–31
Hashing, 29, 31, 83
Hash power, 30
Hash rate, 30
Health records, 68–69
Her Majesty's Land Registry, 58
Hernandez, Juan Orlando, 58
Hexadecimal format, 30
HODL Waves, 33
Honduras, 58, 59
HTTP, 18
Hungary, 5
Hyper-inflation, 46

I
IBM, 34, 88
ID, 73, 84
Identity, 14, 15, 20, 66, 68–71, 73, 75, 95, 96, 98
Immobilise, 63, 94
Immutable, 20, 38, 60, 75, 81
Incentive systems, 36
IncomLend, 85
India, 4, 68, 74, 75, 97n1
Indian Ocean, 83
Institutions of trust, 5, 7, 9, 14, 98
Instituto De La Propiedo (IP), 58
Intermediaries, 9, 11, 15, 17, 18, 103
International Criminal Court (ICC), 20
Internet of things (IoT), 19, 20, 35, 38–40
Invoice Check, 85
IOTA, 39, 40
iPhone, 2, 3
IPOs, 52
ISO, 9

J
JPM Coin, 34, 38
JP Morgan Chase, 34

K
Kenya, 2, 3, 10, 11, 53, 95, 97, 102, 103
Keys, 1, 16, 28, 33, 46, 48, 49, 58, 61, 62, 65, 72, 75, 94, 101
KfW, 67
  TruBudget, 67
Kumasi, 62

L
Lake Malawi, 96
Latin America, 5, 8, 13, 66, 85
Lesotho, 86
Liberia, 5
London Stock Exchange, 15
Lopp, Jameson, 28

M
Madagascar, 83
Malawi, 96
Malaysia, 12
  Ringgit notes, 48
Mastercard, 9
MERJ Exchange, 52, 53

Microsoft, 35
Miners, 29
The Ministry of Weights and Measures, 81
Mobile money, 2–6, 53, 62, 95, 98, 102
Moldova, 86
Monetary Authority of Singapore, 72
Mongolia, 5, 81
Mortgages, 52, 59, 62
Moss-Pultz, Sean, 40
M-Pesa, 2–4, 3n3, 53
Mwinsuubo, Narigamba, 62

N
Nakamoto, Satoshi, 7, 29
Near-Field Communication (NFC), 55
New York, 16
Nigeria, 11, 12, 46, 80, 97
Node operator, 33
Nonce, 30
Non-governmental Organizations (NGO), 94
Notary services, 34, 75

O
OECD, 13
Oil, 9, 34, 82, 83
OmniBnk, 85
Opara, Chibuzo, 80, 80n2
Operators, 31, 33, 97
Oxfam, 66
  Project Unblocked Cash, 66
Oxytocin, 80

P
Pango, 66
Paper money, 9
Papua New Guinea, 6
Patagonia, 42
PayCode, 84
Permissionless, 33, 35, 88
Peru, 75
Pfizer, 68
Philippines, 8, 71, 72
PhilPass, 55
Physical cash, 46, 47, 49, 50, 98
Project i2i, 72
Project Ubin, 72
Proof-of-work, 29–31
Property ownership, 58, 61, 102
Property registers, 10, 34, 96
Public/private key pair, 49

Q
QR code, 35, 80, 82

R
Radical Change, 61
Railways, 4, 70
Reagan, Ronald, 18
Retail, 3, 34, 45, 49
Risk, 1, 2, 9–11, 16–18, 18n5, 20, 32, 38, 46, 48–50, 52, 58, 60, 63, 68, 82–85, 88, 96–98, 102
Risk homeostasis, 17
Rossiello, Elizabeth, 51
Rwanda, 6, 12n1, 35, 75

S
Saudi Aramco, 53
Second World War, 61
Security token, 37
Sempo, 66
Settlement, 47
Seychelles, 52, 53

Shining Path terrorists, 75
Ship Chain, 88
Shnell, Jonas, 28
Sierra Leone, 5
Singapore, 12n1, 72, 85
Smart Contract, 38, 72, 87
SMS, 54
South Asia, 5, 13, 97n1
South-South trade, 85n5, 86, 87
Spotify, 77
Stablecoin, 37, 66
Starbucks, 35
Sub-Saharan Africa, 5, 11, 13, 70, 74, 97n1
Supply chain, 6, 34, 35, 38, 81–85, 88
Swedish state, 64
SWIFT, 55
Swiss Re, 87
Syria, 20
Systems of trust, 58, 93, 98

T

Tadawul, 53
Taiwan, 12n1, 68
Tanzanian Shilling notes, 48
Target, 30, 72
TCP/IP, 18
Technology leapfrogging, 4, 8
Thailand, 6
Timor-Leste, 5
Title insurance, 11, 59, 60
Token, 25, 27, 36, 37, 39, 53, 58, 62, 63, 66, 72
Topl, 84
Torrens system, 59
Trade Finance Market (TFM), 85
TradeLens, 88
Trust, 5, 7–16, 18, 18n5, 19, 25, 36, 58, 62–65, 70, 71, 73, 79, 94, 95, 97, 98, 101
Trustless, 18, 28
Tuohy, Ed, 52
2020 Lome Initiative, 82

U

Uber, 18, 19
Uganda, 6, 35, 83, 84
Ulaanbaatar, 81
UnionBank, 71, 72
  i2i platform, 72
United Kingdom (UK), 2, 3, 12, 58, 63, 75, 94, 102, 103
University of California, Berkeley, 68
U.S. Department of Homeland Security (DHS), 59
US dollar, 8, 33, 36, 46, 51
US Millenniem Challenge Corporation, 64
US monetary policy, 46
Utility token, 36
Uttamchandani, Raj, 85

V

Value-Added Tax (VAT), 96
Van der Laan, Wladimir J., 28
Vanilla, 83
Vanuatu, 66
Venezuela, 12, 46, 51, 97
Visa, 9
VOIP, 18
Volatility, 25, 34, 69, 97
Voting systems, 34, 73

W

Wallet, 2, 16, 33, 39, 48–50, 52
Wall Street, 16
Walmart, 34, 35

WeChat Pay, 3, 4, 18, 19, 38
The World Bank
  Blockchail Lab, 65
  Doing Business project, 11, 13
World Blockchain Trade Consortium (WBTC), 85
World Health Organization (WHO), 80
World Wide Web, 18, 19
Wuille, Pieter, 28

X
XL Catlin, 87

Y
Yehia, Adham, 80, 80n2

Z
Zambia, 57, 84
Zimbabwe, 25, 46, 51, 97
Zurich, 53

9783030517830